Roman Holiday

AMS PRESS

NEW YORK

Roman Holiday

The Catholic Novels of Evelyn Waugh

by A. A. De Vitis

This book was reprinted from a copy in the collections of the Brooklyn Public Library.
Reprinted with permission of Twayne Publishers, Inc.
From the edition of 1956, New York

First AMS edition published 1971
Manufactured in the United States of America

International Standard Book Number: 0-404-02119-0

Library of Congress Catalog Card Number: 71-153314

AMS PRESS INC.
NEW YORK, N.Y, 10003

Contents

Introduction   8

Chapter 1   The Novelist and His Audience   15

Chapter 2   The Early Satire   19

Chapter 3   Later Satire   25

Chapter 4   Roman Catholicism and
             Brideshead Revisited   40

Chapter 5   Towards *Helena* and Church History   54

Chapter 6   Waugh at Arms   68

Chapter 7   Conclusions   82

Bibliography   85

Footnotes   87

depression following upon the inflation and the mad good times of the post-war period. Economic catastrophe was a reality. The early thirties began to bring the threat of still more war. The hopes of Shaw and the Fabians dimmed in the tide of Spanish fascism and German totalitarianism.

In the first quarter of the century, literary concern was with form, style and technique. Virginia Woolf in her criticism rebelled against the naturalism of the nineteenth century, and in *The Common Reader* (1925) she demonstrated clearly her anti-intellectual approach to literature. She preferred to analyze the text in the fashion of the late Romantics, dismissing the Victorian standards of scholarship and history. She watched Mrs. Dalloway through a day in her life and in that one day told her reader all he needed to know concerning her heroine. And Mrs. Dalloway's existence did not include God. She could feel sorry for Septimus Warren Smith, but the causes of his dilemma were primarily psychical, social and economic; God had no place in the pattern of Mrs. Dalloway's thoughts. Lily Briscoe in *To the Lighthouse* (1927) concerned herself with the representation of Mrs. Ramsey as a blob of paint on her canvas. Mrs. Ramsey thought to hold the moment of harmony of the dinner party, and for a second it occurred to her to think of God. Graham Greene has said that the characters of Virginia Woolf "wandered like cardboard symbols through a world that was paper-thin."[2]

E. M. Forster in *Howard's End* (1910) described the philistinism that Matthew Arnold had defined in *Culture and Anarchy*. The Schlegels he represented as Sweetness and Light, and Mr. Wilcox became material progress. In Howard's End, Mrs. Wilcox's home, Forster symbolized the forces of tradition. The unseen presence of Mrs. Wilcox hovering over the house speaks of God, but very obliquely. It is the cultural tradition of Howard's End that is important.

Arnold Bennett and John Galsworthy plodded on in their

Introduction

> I had no religion. I was taken to church weekly as a
> child, and at school attended chapel daily, but, as though
> in compensation, from the time I went to my public
> school I was excused church in the holidays. The view
> implicit in my education was that the basic narrative
> of Christianity had long been exposed as a myth, and
> that opinion was now divided as to whether its ethical
> teaching was of present value, a division in which the
> main weight went against it; religion was a hobby
> which some people professed and others did not; at
> the best it was slightly ornamental, at the worst it was
> the province of "complexes" and "inhibitions"—catch
> words of the decade—and of the intolerance, hypocrisy,
> and sheer stupidity attributed to it for centuries.[1]

The nineteenth century left to the twentieth a growing
uneasiness in the face of the materialistic advances of science
and the rising influence of the middle class. Moral and
political ideas succumbed to the influence of Lenin and
Marx, and the human personality found itself subjected to
the analyses of Jung and Freud. T. S. Eliot detected a death
wish in western civilization, defined it, and set forth the most
comprehensive set of symbols for characterizing the period
of the early years of the century. Few serious thinkers were
able to maintain orthodox belief in the face of all this confusion and turmoil. There was no place to turn, and it became fashionable to have oneself psychoanalyzed in order
to understand how the personality reflected the order of the
day. In the late twenties and early thirties there came a

realistic fashion, but their realism seemed to imply no God in the world. *The Forsyte Saga—The Man of Property* first appeared in 1906—moved the Forsytes out of the Victorian era, through the Edwardian lull, and into a twentieth century in which not even Soames's property was valuable any longer. *The Old Wives' Tale* (1908) described two women and traced their development in mundane realistic description that occasionally sprang into a vitality all its own. But neither Sophia nor Constance paid any more than lip service to God.

A few like D. H.. Lawrence reacted violently against the severe and unfeeling strictures of nineteenth-century religion. In his rebellion were contained the seeds of his religious search. He sought to revitalize religion by returning to the springs of feeling. He looked in *The Plumed Serpent* (1926) for king-gods; and in *The Man Who Died* (1928) he took over the Christ myth and infused his own ideas of sex into it. Christ, he decided, had not been a whole man because he had not found his polarity in woman. So Lawrence raised Him from the tomb and sent Him out searching for a complement. In the art and life of the Etruscans Lawrence found the epitome of civilization represented; and it was their appreciation of life, of vitality, of meaningful existence that he attempted to incorporate into his final work. Occasionally the desire to shock the complacent was too strong for him, and he wrote *Lady Chatterley's Lover* (1928). Lawrence traveled the world looking for a race still expressive of dark and vital blood; in Mexico he thought he found untrammelled feelings and vital meaning springing from a belief in the ancient gods. Lawrence's search was a real one. Having inherited the disillusionment of the nineteenth century, he felt it necessary to find a substitute religion. That which he formulated, unfortunately, most people found distasteful, choosing to misunderstand his exaltation of sex.

In Ireland James Joyce rejected Irish Catholicism, and

by doing so he turned himself, paradoxically, into the most Catholic of writers. In *A Portrait of the Artist as a Young Man* (1916) he traced his own spiritual awareness in the character of Stephen Dedalus; and like Stephen, Joyce concluded that to remain faithful to his artistic vision he would have to leave Ireland. *Ulysses* (1926), his magnificent *tour de force*, was created in terms of classical myth; it traced Stephen's rebellion against his God and his country still further. Into *Ulysses* Joyce put all the paraphernalia of psychoanalysis stemming from Jung and Freud and fused it with a stream-of-consciousness technique; and once and for all he indicated the limitations of that device in the soliloquies of Mollie and Leopold Bloom.

The writers of the thirties picked up some loose threads of idealism and began to take stock. A group of poets looked about them and saw to what a monstrous size the social organism had grown. W. H. Auden, Stephen Spender, and C. Day Lewis began to advocate English socialism. They preached de-centralization of industry so that the social unit might be made smaller and man might again communicate with man. They sought to revitalize the poetic metaphor by drawing images from the machine itself, and they tried to re-educate the masses to understand the dangers of capitalism. They claimed their literary descent from Gerard Manley Hopkins, T. S. Eliot, Wilfred Owen, and D. H. Lawrence. From the ruins of nineteenth-century pessimism that had led man to wish for death in the twentieth century, they sought for new meaning, for a new order. They looked for a way out of the waste land. Eliot in his poetry had defined the era; they took up the battle from there. Meanwhile, Eliot clarified his beliefs in his literary criticism.

In *After Strange Gods* (1934) Eliot showed himself aware of the confusion apparent in the writings of the nineteenth century. He praised George Eliot for her insights into human motivations, but he deplored her individualistic morals. He insisted that the writer to be faithful to society had to remain within an orthodox conception of tradition and history:

> What I have been leading up to is the following assertion: that when morals cease to be a matter of tradition and orthodoxy—that is, of the habits of the community formulated, corrected, and elevated by the continuous thought and direction of the Church—and when each man is to elaborate his own, then *personality* becomes a thing of alarming importance.[3]

He found Thomas Hardy's emotionalism a symptom of decadence, for Hardy's personality was "uncurbed by any institutional attachment or by submission to any objective beliefs. . . ."[*After Strange Gods*, 54] And he deplored Lawrence's eccentricity in setting up for himself a system of gods opposed to the Church. In other words, Eliot asserted the validity of the orthodox teachings of the Church. He found in the cumulative wisdom of the Church the answers to the ills of the waste land; and in dogma he found a measure upon which to base one's spiritual awareness. As far as the artist in society is concerned, Eliot saw it necessary for him to point out the differences between good and evil, and he insisted that awakening men to the spiritual life was a great responsibility: "It is only when they are so awakened that they are capable of real Good, but . . . at the same time they first become capable of Evil." [*After Strange Gods*, 60] The artist is made aware that art cannot exist for itself alone.

The orthodox teachings of the Church found very real opponents in the political theories prevalent in the thirties. William York Tindall in *Forces in Modern British Literature: 1885–1946* described the influences that marked English literature since the First World War:

> Disenchantment and its effects, the cynical, the disgusting, and the grotesque, though products of the first World War, existed before it as products of science

and bourgeois self-contemplation. With these effects
came others, the comic, the ironic, and the fantastic, the
last of which appears an attempt of the disenchanted to
rediscover enchantment. Attitudes of disenchantment,
found at their happiest in the work of Huxley and young
Waugh, occur so abundantly that, like politics and religion, they discover the times.[4]

The thirties continued to lament a world in which physics
had displaced metaphysics. The return to the Church, paral-
leling the trend to Communism and Socialism, indicated a
desire to evaluate clearly matter and spirit. It indicated that
perhaps religion was catching up with science. The real
opponents to a religion that offered ways and means of re-
uniting matter with spirit were the Fascists and the Com-
munists.

André Gide best typifies the attitude that opposed the
march back to the Church. In Arachon on the tenth of
August, 1933, he wrote in his journal:

> The great grievance one can have against the Chris-
> tian religion is that it sacrifices the strong to the weak.
> But that strength should strive to find its function in
> bringing help to weakness, how can one fail to approve
> this?[5]

The conflict was between a cult of power and a religion of
love. To approve the teachings of the Church and sub-
scribe to the teachings of Marx and Lenin seemed impossible,
for love and violence are totally incompatible. Communism
advocated strength and the strong man; whereas a capitalis-
tic system allowed for meekness and humility. Capitalism
could strike the oppressed a blow on the cheek, and religion
could ask him to turn the other cheek, soothing him with
promises of retribution in an after-life. Yet capitalism and
religion accepted the past, and even André Gide was forced
to admit that there was value in tradition and that systems

which endeavored to build by destroying had their limitations:

> For it is absurd to try to condemn, in the name of the future, all the past; and not to realize, in this case as everywhere else a filiation, a succession, and that the spirit which drives them, more or less oppressed, has never ceased to exist. . . The vision of these young haters of today seems to me limited. Nothing will age more rapidly than their modernism: it is only by thrusting out from a foothold in the past that the present can spring into the future. [*Journals*, III, 226]

This statement coming from the advocate of the gratuitous act, the act committed for no real reason save the gratification of the individual lust, reveals how far Gide had gone since his earliest works. The reliance on tradition—although Gide would never agree with the teachings of any church—indicates that in his maturity he came to realize the necessity for restricting individual conduct.

The Church, then, offered again a basis for real meaning in the world to those who would accept its teachings. Not only that, but religion suddenly became popular. Psychoanalysis found a close rival in ritual and worship. It became fashionable to be converted to either Anglicanism or Roman Catholicism. One was required to be *savant* in the forms of religion to be in the literary swing. What is important, however, is that those writers who wrote about God and tradition took their work seriously. They wrote for society, and they had a message to deliver. The message was from God, and it indicated how man could put his garden to rights and reclaim the desert waste it had become since science had moved God out of the universe. Aldous Huxley, Rex Warner, J. B. Priestley, Christopher Isherwood, Graham Greene, Auden, Spender and many others fell into a pattern of conversion. Following a path outlined by T. S. Eliot, using the imagery and motifs of *The Waste Land,* they looked about them and understood that their function as writers was a serious one. They used the stuff of their religious convictions as the basis for their works. And they succeeded in creating some of the most compelling literature of our times.

Evelyn Waugh, the second son of Arthur Waugh and the brother of Alec Waugh, was born in 1903. His early career included work on the *Daily Express* and a venture in school teaching. In 1928 he married Evelyn Gardner from whom he was divorced in 1930; and in 1937 he married Laura Herbert. His first book of note was a study of Dante Gabriel Rossetti, published in 1928. This was followed by *Decline and Fall,* a novel, and by several travelogues, records of his voyages to Ethiopia and Mexico. In 1930 he joined the Roman Catholic Church, and in 1935 his study of Edmund Campion, the Catholic martyr, appeared. Waugh joined the British Army as a commando in 1939 and, at present, makes his permanent home at Stinchcombe in England.

Chapter 1

The Novelist
and His Audience

Jacques Maritain, speaking within the defined limits of Thomistic philosophy, discusses in *Art and Scholasticism* the problem of evil in the world and the novelist's responsibility to his audience. The novelist's purpose, he says, is not to mirror life as the painter does but to create the experience of it. The novel, of course, derives its rules of conduct from the real world, but its integrity as a work of art depends upon the quality of the experience of human life which it creates. "The object it has to create is human life itself. . . ."[6] It becomes the concern of the reader to understand the novelist's intention, to know with what object he portrays the aspects of evil:

> The essential question is *from what altitude* he depicts and whether his art and mind are pure enough and strong enough to depict it without connivance. The more deeply the modern novelist probes human misery, the more does it require super-human virtues in the novelist. [Maritain, 171]

There are two important observations made in this passage. The first concerns the artist who embodies within the limitations of his own genius a world as complete and as whole as possible. The embodiment of this world is a difficult task, something from the great Schism and the Reformation. This proposition seemed so plain to me that it admitted of no discussion. It only remained to examine the historical and philosophic grounds for supposing Christian revelation to be genuine.[7]

In his personal life Waugh sought for the order and integrity of tradition, and this tradition he found in the Catholic Church. No longer attractive because of its extreme rationalism, the agnosticism of the nineteeenth century gave way before the demand for assurance and definite belief.[8]

Chapter 2

The Early Satire

William York Tindall in *Forces in Modern British Literature* accepts the idea of Waugh's removal from the world of his creation, but this removal he finds the true expression of the artistic spirit:

> Like Huxley, Waugh found in religion a refuge from the world and a point of view from which to regard it; but unlike Huxley he remained an artist, leaving sermons to the clergy. His public religion, improving his art, gave to his moralities intensity and that monkish loathing by which he pleases. [Tindall, 123]

This "monkish loathing" amounts, indeed, to an active sense of evil in the real world, a sense of evil derived from the appreciation of a deeply felt religious conviction. In *Decline and Fall* (1928) Waugh traced the lives of the Bright Young People insanely seeking a good time in the period following the First World War. His attitude in the novel was primarily a secular one. He did not sermonize. Nor did he merely describe. He aimed his acid wit at his characters, making them make themselves ridiculous. The moral commentary was oblique, and the religious convictions that were to inform *Brideshead Revisited* were not at all portrayed in either character or action. In his representation of the hysteria that characterized the period in England and on the Continent, Waugh succeeded in creating the British counterpart of the

American jazz age described in more flamboyant fashion in the novels of Hemingway, Fitzgerald and O'Hara.

In *Decline and Fall* the satire was aimed principally at institutions. First Waugh poked fun at English boys' schools, then he directed his wit at British penal conventions, and finally he moved into a satire of British government and politics as represented by the portly Lord Metroland. All the while he made his nasty comments about the Bright Young People, for whom he felt a strange concern. His wit and his malice were perfectly directed. He scored a hit at every turn. Yet he managed to delight his readers because somehow he implied to them that they were above this sort of thing. This he did by means of his hero, Paul Pennyfeather. In the character of his hero Waugh managed to create a link between himself and the real world and to make an offhand commentary on the actions of his sophisticated and depraved characters. Professor Silenus says to Paul at the end of the novel:

"People don't see that when they say 'life' they mean two different things. They can mean simply existence, with its physiological implications of growth and organic change. They can't escape that—even by death, but because that's inevitable they think the other idea of life is too—the scrambling and the excitement and bumps and the effort to get to the middle, and when we do get to the middle, it's just as if we never started. It's so odd.

"Now you're a person who was clearly meant to stay in the seats and sit still and if you get bored watch the others. Somehow you got on the wheel, and you got thrown off again with a hard bump. It's all right for Margot, who can cling on, and for me, at the centre, but you're static. Instead of this absurd division into sexes they ought to class people as static and dynamic. There's a real distinction there, though I can't tell you how it comes." [9]

Paul Pennyfeather is passive rather than static. Without any knowledge of the "real" world represented by Margot Beste-Chetwynde, he finds himself drafted from his theological studies to become her lover. Innocently, passively, he becomes involved in her white slavery enterprise, is put in prison, is allowed to "escape" by means of pressures and bribes in the right places. He returns to his theological studies, sporting a new beard and none the worse for wear.

In Paul, Waugh demonstrates how untenable in a modern, frenzied world are the moral and ethical codes of the Victorian period, a theme he will develop later on in the more complex *A Handful of Dust* (1934). Paul insists on taking the blame for Margot's unlawful enterprises, and she rewards him by first marrying Lord Metroland and then taking Alastair Vaine-Digby Trumpington as her lover.

Decline and Fall derives its vitality, paradoxically, not from Paul Pennyfeather but from the two-dimensional characters who exist without benefit of direct moral commentary from their author. They convince the reader of their comic worth while moving hysterically across the pages of the novel. Captain Grimes contrives against Mr. Prendergast; Lady Circumference moves from one party to another; Margot from one lover to another; Peter Pastmaster at twelve smokes cigarettes, mixes his own drinks and chooses his mother's lovers. Waugh's universe is indeed an extension of Eliot's waste land. In a world that has forgotten God there can be little comfort for anyone who thinks seriously about nature and about life. To keep an equilibrium, one develops a sense of the ridiculous and one exploits it. This is Waugh's triumph.

The problem of Waugh's comic genius in his novels before *Brideshead Revisited* cannot, however, be solved so easily as this. If the idea of the novelist's removal from the world of his invention is accepted, then the definition of moral purpose is a tenuous matter, and as with Waugh, the

comic convention can further complicate the situation. For
from the first novel on, the characters have strength and
vitality. The plot incidents are at once cruel and uproarious.
Little Lord Tangent, Lady Circumference's son, is shot in the
foot by an assistant master. There are periodic remarks made
as to his progress—the foot's gangrene, its amputation, and
finally, the death of the boy. Yet the entire sequence is
extremely funny in the context of the novel, so funny indeed
that the moral implications are temporarily defeated. One
must return to Paul Pennyfeather and those like him to
attack the heart of the problem.

D. S. Savage in "The Innocence of Evelyn Waugh" discusses the novelist's removal from his characters in this way:

> The world of human experience is held at such a dis-
> tance as to preclude the possibility of its being taken
> seriously; at a distance at which persons become puppets
> and thereby appropriate objects of diversion.[10]

This is not altogether true. The satire of such a novel as
Decline and Fall is aimed at institutions and at men and
women. Perhaps the comic elements are so persuasive that
they obscure the oblique moral commentary. According to
Savage, the removal from the world of his creation engenders
in Waugh's work a comedy of innocence. The hero becomes
an innocent observer of society. And his innocence amounts
to an inability to grow up:

> I think that centrally Waugh reveals the predicament of
> immaturity. He is the brilliant undergraduate who has
> difficulty in growing up. As a comic writer he remains
> at a distance from experience which he views with a
> premature cynicism; as a serious novelist he endeavors
> to comprehend experience but is prevented by the mists
> of sentiment exhaled from a childish or adolescent in-
> nocence which has never, really, been outgrown. Like so

many sophisticates, Waugh is at bottom romantically idealist. His conservatism which some have called neo-fascist, is merely the desire for the perpetuation of a social pattern known and loved in childhood and youth: his patent dislike for the workers and his obvious snobbery are symptoms of the narrowed human sympathy which results from a failure in growth. [Savage, 35]

This is much too harsh an analysis. There is some truth in Savage's observations, but on the whole he exaggerates both the immaturity and the snobbery. If Waugh is "romantically idealist," then his satire should be more readily understandable, but his preoccupation with innocence does offer an understanding of the satirical method.

It is quite apparent that Waugh's interest in the aspects of immaturity and his understanding of the adolescent mind afford him his greatest latitude in his satirical portraits of society. But the problem inevitably resolves itself into a consideration of the point from which he views the world of his creation. The position of the innocent is relative to this point, as is that of the reader at whom the novel is directed. Paul Pennyfeather in *Decline and Fall* borders on the fool, although it would be completely incorrect to label him one. His genuine naiveté makes him a prey to the workings of the impatient society represented by Margot and her precocious son, Peter. Waugh's sympathy—and the reader's—is for Paul. And Paul's failure is an inability to make a moral evaluation of the society he is thrown into. His position as pawn in the hands of forces his innocence makes him incapable of understanding allows Waugh to portray with all the malicious wit at his command that evil which culminates in Margot's white slavery trade. Paul escapes with nothing worse than a "hard bump." By the end of the novel the experiences of his youth are over; he has resumed his theological studies.

Into a setting of high life and pseudo-sophistication Waugh places an individual spiritually unequipped to understand the evil of the world. This innocence is ironical. And it serves as a leaven. The issues involved in the presentation of the theme rise to prominence because of him. His observations are provoked not by outside motives but by inner convictions which he may not understand himself; for this character seems apart from the surface action of the novel, although, ironically, it centers upon what he does. In *Decline and Fall* Paul Pennyfeather is told what to do by his mistress. He cannot comprehend the sordidness of her trade, but passively he is propelled by it. Yet he is neither corrupted nor corroded by the experience. Something inside himself keeps him basically the same person at the novel's end that he was at its beginning. His innocence is tougher than life. Since at times this hero plays the fool, he succeeds in underscoring the irony; his very foolishness, a portion of his innocence, establishes the moral perspective. He becomes the link between the author and the real world. The innocence of this character is a potent influence; his ironic compassion excites the humanity of the reader who, in turn, feels the force of innocence as part of the structure of society. The innocence maintains the balance between the secular and the religious world.

Chapter 3

Later Satire

On first looking into Waugh, Edmund Wilson was impressed with his "ingenious audacity and breath-taking spontaneity." [11] In *Vile Bodies* (1930) Wilson discovered a standard of measurement from which to judge the works. This he found in the portrayal of Anchorage House as a symbol of the dying aristocracy of England, an aristocracy characterized by grace and dignity and other-worldliness; by marked eccentricities too. Wilson originally saw Waugh as a creator standing outside his world and gauging it from the standards of British nobility; and with this attitude of snobbery he completely concurred. Waugh's universe was for him a completely contrived one, a world that existed by virtue of its spontaneity and audacity. He ascribed Waugh's success in those novels before *Brideshead Revisited* to the fact that there were no political or moral judgments made. He wrote:

> About this fiction there is nothing schematic and nothing doctrinaire; and, though the characters are often stock types—the silly ass, the vulgar parvenu, the old clubman, etc.—everything in it has grown out of experience and everything has emotional value. . . It is the satisfying expression of the artist, whose personal pattern of feeling no formula will ever fit, whether political, social or moral. For the savagery he is afraid of is somehow the same thing as the audacity which so delights him. [Wilson, 146]

With the publication of *Brideshead Revisited,* however, Wilson approached the judgment of Waugh's craft with a definite bias. He readily admitted his lack of sympathy for the convert to Roman Catholicism; but for all his bias his criticism was as astute as before it had been appreciative:

> . . . Waugh's snobbery, hitherto held in check by his satirical point of view, has here emerged shameless and rampant. His admiration for the qualities of the older British families, as contrasted with modern up-starts, had its value in his earlier novels, where standards of morals and taste are kept in the background and merely implied. But here the upstarts are rather crudely overdone and the aristocrats become terribly trashy, and his cult of the high nobility is allowed to become so rapturous and so solemn that it finally gives the impression of being the only only real religion in the book. [Wilson, 300]

Waugh's earlier novels had succeeded brilliantly by virtue of their separation from the world of real life. The ties had been slight and barely discernible. The rules of the game were Waugh's. He wrote from an "altitude" which Wilson correctly diagnosed as snobbery. In Waugh's refusal to either apologize for or explain the actions of his characters, he saw the basis of the novels' success. How Wilson could have read *A Handful of Dust,* called it Waugh's masterpiece, examined the epigraph from Eliot, and failed to appreciate the moral, even religious, implications of the theme is another problem. But Wilson did notice that with each novel Waugh approached closer and closer to the customs of conventional fiction. In the knowledge of Waugh's development up to *Brideshead Revisited,* he saw Waugh coming slowly down from the heights, inevitably approaching a definite statement of his convictions, a serious consideration of the real world. In *Brideshead* Waugh found it necessary to speak seriously on a serious subject, to expand into a new dimension and, paradoxically, into the traditional form of the novel.

Before *Brideshead Revisited* Waugh had been content to portray the chaotic world of the thirties; he had created his own waste land. He looked at the doings of Peter Pastmaster, Margot Metroland, John Beaver and Polly Cockpurse from his vantage point of moral superiority, and his snobbery found expression in his use of the upper classes as the main exponents of his story's action. Since the religious and moral implications were not permitted to find explicit voice in the main action of the themes, the satire became pointed and devastating, remote as it seemed from any moral frame of reference. Wilson characterized this removal as "perverse, unregenerate self-will, giving rise to confusion and impudence . . ." [Wilson, 301] In *Vile Bodies* Waugh chose Father Rothschild S. J. and Mrs. Melrose Ape, together with her troop of angels, Charity, Fortitude, Chastity and Creative Endeavor, as examples of the moral corruption of the times. Rothschild, the wealthy, worldly Jesuit, thinks of the saints, the mutability of human nature, the Four Last Things and recites snatches of the psalms while listening to Mrs. Ape's angels sing, "There ain't no flies on the Lamb of God." Father Rothschild comments on the workings of the Bright Young People in this way:

> "Don't you think . . . that it is all in some way historical? I don't think that people ever *want* to lose their faith either in religion or anything else. I know very few young people, but it seems to me that they are all possessed with an almost fatal hunger for permanence. People aren't content to just muddle along nowadays . . . They won't make the best of a bad job nowadays. . . . They say, 'If a thing's not worth doing well, it's not worth doing at all.' It makes everything very difficult for them." [12]

This is an excellent estimate of the times. Nineteenth-century science having deprived the world of faith, of God, there is nothing tangible to hold on to. A world catastrophe has awakened the death wish in western civilization, and another catastrophe is foreshadowed. All that is left is a good time. And Father Rothschild admits, ironically, that perhaps the Bright Young People are right. Into this world of Agatha Runcibles and Alastair Trumpingtons and Simon Balcairns comes Adam Fenwyk-Symes, in his confused way seeking permanence in a marriage to Nina Blount. But this permanence he never achieves, for Nina marries a man with money, and Adam becomes her lover:

> "Adam, darling, what's the matter?"
> "I don't know . . . Nina do you ever feel that things simply can't go on much longer?"
> "What d' you mean by things—us or everything?"
> "Everything."
>
>   ❂   ❂   ❂
>
> Later he said: "I'd give anything in the world for something different."
> "Different from me or from everything?"
> "Different from everything . . . only I've got nothing . . . what's the good of talking?" [*Vile Bodies*, 185]

Here, as Father Rothschild has accurately analyzed, the character who is the innocent in the action desires the permanence whose lack results in a pointless existence—which leads another character to death in a frenzied attempt to have a good time while recuperating from a serious automobile accident. The commentary on the state of the world is made by Adam; and he sees correctly that the gay, sophisticated existence of the young people is meaningless. There is nothing to give meaning to it. And Adam is little better than those around him. He sells Nina to his rival for seventy-eight pounds, sixteen and twopence and goes off to find excite-

ment in a pointless and fantastic war. Yet *Vile Bodies* gives
evidence through Adam Symes of a closer awareness of the
emptiness that characterized the times immediately following the First World War. Adam's war is a nightmare fantasy
that captures the disillusionment of the period. Paul Pennyfeather had been content to go back to his theological studies,
untarnished by his exploits with Margot Metroland; but
Adam, somewhat wiser than Paul, sees the futility of an
existence whose very worthlessness forms the basis of uncomfortably funny situations.

In *Black Mischief* (1932) the innocence that characterized Paul Pennyfeather and Adam Symes finds a strange
expression in the character of Basil Seal. In him Waugh prefers to examine the qualities of childhood which are boister-
ous, cruel and often sadistic. These traits are presented with
a blasé self-assurance as Waugh moves into an East African
principality and such intrigues as a civil war, a Birth Control
parade and, finally, a cannibal feast. The previous two heroes
had been passive creatures involved in situations which they
could not completely understand, and they managed to re-
tain much of their original simplicity at the novels' end. In
presenting through Basil Seal the exuberant, impetuous
activity of youth without direction, Waugh creates in effect
the portrait of a bounder. D. S. Savage points out that his
portrait of the *enfant terrible* renders Basil immune to the
contagion of society; for all his ceaseless activity amounts to
nothing more than inertia, "because he has removed himself
from feeling in order to stand over and exploit the external
world." [Savage, 39] *Black Mischief*, in picturing the life of
a remote African principality, makes its appeal primarily on
the basis of snobbery: the white man's racial superiority is
the bias that cuts across the novel's action. The comedy is
not particularly effective in this case because the author's
ties with the real world are closer than they had been in the
preceding books. There is a need for apology and explana-

tion. But the satire is not blunted by any means; it appears uncomfortably closer. The descriptions of the reactions of the Anglican, Catholic and Nestorian churches of Azazia to the Emperor Seth's projected Birth Control and Sterility drive bring into relief Waugh's opinions concerning the problem:

> Now, on the question of Birth Control, his Beatitude left the faithful in no doubt as to where their duty lay. As the head of the Established Church he called a conference which was attended by the Chief Rabbi, the Mormon Elder and the chief representatives of all the creeds of the Empire; only the Anglican Bishop excused himself, remarking in a courteous letter of refusal, that his work lay exclusively among the British community who, since they were already fully informed and equipped in the matter, could scarcely be injured in any way by the Emperor's new policy . . .[13]

Even the fervor of the enthusiastic Basil cools in the face of the Emperor's insane manipulations of the government: "It was on that afternoon that Basil at last lost his confidence in the permanence of the One Year Plan." [*Black Mischief*, 153]

The bounderism that is portrayed in this character forces Waugh to examine more acutely the issues involved in the satire. It becomes apparent that he is still looking at his universe from an "altitude," but the "altitude" is not as removed as it had been before. *Black Mischief* is not a completely successful novel: the exuberance and the seeming illogicality of the first two novels are present in the London scenes describing Alastair and Sonia Trumpington, but this society is not so marvelous and full of gusto as it had been before. The blasé Angela Lyne, in love with Basil, lacks the sparkle and impetuosity of her predecessor, Nina Blount. She is stylized out of all spontaneity. The African scenes, furthermore, because they do rely for their comic value on snob appeal and on racial prejudice, very often fall through. Depravity appears more often as depravity, not as comic invention.

A Handful of Dust returns to the theme of the innocent, but unlike _Decline and Fall_ and _Vile Bodies_, it is more nearly a serious treatment of the society of the thirties. Tony Last, the hero of the piece, is much the same innocent that Paul Pennyfeather and Adam Symes had been, except that he is overcome by the decadent world he refuses to understand. Unlike his predecessors, who possessed nothing, Tony Last is the owner of a great house—Hetton Abbey; and as such he has a responsibility to understand the world within which the house exists. Yet Hetton Abbey is not a bulwark against the materialism of the world; it is a refuge from it.

In Tony Last, Waugh creates a hero whose nostalgia for the romantic past finds expression in his every action. The rooms of the Victorian Gothic Abbey are appropriately named after the members of the Arthurian courts—Guinevere, Lancelot, Galahad and others. The central theme of the novel is one of infidelity. The novel, dealing as it does with marriage, brings Waugh quite near to the world of real men. A serious consideration of the position of Last in the fast-moving, meaningless world of Polly Cockpurse, Jenny Abdul-Akbar and Mrs. Beaver allows him to cut through the veneer of sophistication and to develop his theme in all its inhuman aspects. Tony lives in Hetton Abbey, a Gothic monster of an estate, and he dreams of restoring it to the position of baronial prestige it held in the nineteenth century. Innocent, happy in the habit of trusting his wife, Tony insists on living in the Tennysonian world of _The Idylls of the King_. The standards of Victorian architecture and those of Victorian morality are, however, out of date. This Gothic world falls to pieces, and he comes to understand fear in his handful of dust. Tony now has nothing left, not even the comfort of religion. After the death of his son, John Andrew, Tony had said to Mrs. Rattery, the Shameless Blonde, "[After] all the last thing one wants to talk about at a time like this is religion." And the Shameless Blonde had answered, "Some like it." [14]

In the death of John Andrew, Waugh satirizes the secular attitude to death, a theme which he will develop in *The Loved One*. Tony sees in the death of the boy only the extinction of life. There is no core of religious understanding in his philosophy to give meaning to death. He rightly understands that no one is to blame for his son's death—no one in particular. But everyone in general is guilty—Brenda, Tony, the world. With the death of John Andrew the Victorian dream comes to an end. Tony is the last of his kind, as his name implies. Brenda finds no more reason to remain his wife, and she seeks a divorce. Guinevere has betrayed Arthur; but Lancelot has degenerated into John Beaver, a kept man.

In his search for the lost city, the purpose of his Brazilian adventure, Tony looks for another confirmation of his romantic dream. As Tony dreams of the lost splendors of Hetton, hunting for its replica in the jungles of Brazil, Waugh makes reference to the theme of the city in *The Waste Land*, and he implies that the city Tony seeks is the city of God. The references, however, are oblique and cannot be pressed. On reaching the house of Mr. Todd, the illiterate half-breed, Tony, in his delirium, voices his belief in gentleness, the gentleness in him that had made him unable to cope with the problems of the waste land, the gentleness that amounted to inertia:

> Listen to me. I know that I am not clever but that is no
> reason why we should all forget courtesy. Let us kill in
> the gentlest manner. I will tell you what I have learned
> in the forest, where time is different. There is no City.
> Mrs. Beaver has covered it with chromium plating and
> converted it into flats . . . Very suitable for base love.

And Polly will be there. She and Mrs. Beaver under the
fallen battlements. . . . [*A Handful of Dust*, 225]

Once he understands that his years will be spent reading
Dickens to the mad native, Tony is completely overwhelmed
by the world of Lady Cockpurse. It is essentially ironic that
the first novel Mr. Todd pulls off the shelf is *Bleak House*,
the most Gothic of Dickens' works.

A *Handful of Dust* is important in a consideration of
Waugh's development for several reasons. First of all, it is
the transitional novel between his "secular" or comic works
and his "religious" novels beginning with *Brideshead Revisited*. Secondly, the novel states Waugh's belief in the
responsibility of the aristocracy. Through Anchorage House
and Hetton Abbey he portrays his belief in the traditions of
the aristocracy as a link between the present and the meaningful past. Thirdly, the book reveals Waugh coming closer
to the real world, and the more conventional forms of the
novel, in his investigation of marital infidelity. Anthony Last
is the author's link with his reader, and the expression, "Hard
Cheese on Tony," becomes the chorus accompanying the
action and arousing the humanity of the audience. Fourthly,
the novel is important because it demonstrates that fundamental innocence, while in itself a virtue, must understand
its polarity—evil; otherwise it will be overcome. Overcome,
but not destroyed, for it is tougher than life. Tony, though
lost to the world and to Brenda, lives on, his living death the
result of his inability to understand the complexities of the
world he has left behind. The ironical conclusion is the only
possible one, after considering the implications of the plot.
Fifthly, and most important of all, the background of all
Waugh's work is brought clearly into focus—the waste land
of Eliot's poem. The religious implications begin to demand
explicit statement.

Scoop (1938), like *Black Mischief*, makes a bald appeal

to the white man's sense of racial superiority. The novel is loosely allegorical as it follows the pattern of the Italian invasion into Ethiopia. The question of Communist, Fascist and imperialistic aggression is neatly satirized in the chaos that prevails in the African state of Ishmaelia:

> You see they are all negroes. And the fascists won't be called black because of their racial pride, so they are called White after the White Russians. And the Bolshevists *want* to be called black because of *their* racial pride. So when you *say* black you mean red, and when you *mean* red you say white and when the party who call themselves blacks say traitors they mean what *we* call blacks, but what *we* mean when we say traitors I really couldn't tell you.[15]

The hero of the novel, William Boot, is the author of "Lush Places," an animal column published in the *Daily Beast*. He is mistakenly chosen to represent Lord Cooper's newspaper as foreign correspondent in Ishmaelia. In his passive way he succeeds in making himself a people's hero. William Boot is a descendant of the innocent who had been portrayed in *Decline and Fall* and *Vile Bodies* and, to a certain extent, in *A Handful of Dust*. Boot is content to live in his family house along with his ancient and eccentric relatives who adhere, more or less, to the ethic of their own, the Victorian, period. The mistake engendered in the Fleet Street newspaper office places Boot in an alien environment to which he endeavors to adapt himself; but all the while he prefers the Victorian comforts of Boot Magna and the pleasures of his own room:

> An oddly-placed, square window rising shoulder height from the low wainscot, fringed outside with ivy, brushed by the boughs of a giant monkey-puzzle; a stretch of faded wallpaper on which hung a water color of the

village churchyard painted in her more active days by
Miss Scope, a small shelf of ill assorted books and a
stuffed ferret, whose death from rat poisoning had over-
shadowed the whole of one Easter holiday from his
private school—these, according as he woke on his right
or left side, greeted William daily at Boot Magna.
[*Scoop*, 35]

Like his predecessors William Boot lives in the nostalgic
past, his happy days of childhood. All that he wants is at
Boot Magna. And in the description of the house, Waugh
obliquely makes reference to the great house as a bulwark
of traditions in themselves valid, but outmoded in practice.

Unlike Paul Pennyfeather and Adam Symes, William
Boot has an important decision to make in *Scoop*. He must
decide whether, after his success as a foreign correspondent,
he will remain in the world of affairs and abandon his innocent and happy pursuits or continue his private and unevent-
ful existence at Boot Magna. He decides to do the latter,
but in arranging his life accordingly, he allows the world,
represented by the *Daily Beast* and all the Megopolitan
enterprises, to outwit itself; for Boot continues to write his
column, "Lush Places," at an income of two thousand pounds
a year, happy in his researches on the great-crested grebe.

Scoop, on the whole, is not a successful novel. It is hastily
assembled and exhibits many of the characteristics of a pot-
boiler. The love affair seems completely out of keeping with
the main action, and often the scenes are too contrived to be
funny. Often Waugh strains for his comic effect. The novel
is, however, important when considered alongside *Brideshead Revisited*, inasmuch as it, like *A Handful of Dust*, gives
evidence of Waugh's dependence on the traditions of the
aristocracy to bolster the individual's courage against the
insanities of the modern waste land. The concern with the
innocent as a pawn in a comic drama of international intrigue indicates, too, a closer understanding and awareness

of the social scene. The fact that William Boot retains his innocence at the novel's end while beating the career-struck world at its own game, the fact that he prefers the eccentricities of his own home to the inane success of the world, indicates an optimistic note, a note that emerges predominant for the first time. For at the end of his adventures he is happier and wiser in his innocence. Tony Last had been wiser and sadder, but too late. His passivity had brought on an ending to the novel that is at once tragic and ironical. Boot refuses to take any further part in the commerce of society because he has nothing of value to sell; the best he can do is retire and secure his own integrity. For nothing will equip him to live in the chaotic universe represented by the *Daily Beast*. William is incapable of coping with the forces he has come to understand. To invade the world he would need a banner, and the banner that flies over Boot Magna is in tatters. It is left to Guy Crouchback to invade the world under a banner still whole enough to demand the allegiance of the many.

Put Out More Flags (1942) is an interesting stage in Waugh's over-all development because in it he takes a formal leave of those characters and their world that had preoccupied him since *Decline and Fall*. In the Dedication to Randolph Churchill he writes:

> I am afraid that these pages may not be altogether acceptable to your ardent and sanguine nature. They deal, mostly, with a race of ghosts, the survivors of the world we both knew ten years ago, which you have out-flown in the empyrean of strenuous politics, but where my imagination still fondly lingers. I find more food for thought in the follies of Basil Seal and Ambrose Silk, than in the sagacity of higher command. These characters are no longer contemporary in sympathy; they were forgotten even before the war; but they lived on delightfully in holes and corners and, like everyone else, they

have been disturbed in their habits by the rough intrusion of current history. Here they are in that odd, dead period before the Churchillian renaissance, which people called at the time the Great Bore War.[16]

Margot Metroland, Peter Pastmaster, Basil Seal, Alastair Trumpington and Ambrose Silk are neatly disposed of so that Waugh may in the future consider more "strenuous" problems.

Basil Seal, the *enfant terrible* of *Black Mischief*, is immediately dedicated to the war effort by his sister, his mistress and his mother. They feel that the war alone affords a scope sufficient for the development of his potentialities. Basil refuses, however, to share in their enthusiasm since he fondly holds on to his childhood dream that someone high up in official circles will approach him, speak to him of the necessity of complete dedication to the cause of England in war, offer him an important and dangerous post, and allow him to develop all the cunning and skill that society had hitherto considered flaws in his character. But Basil is a grown man, too old for such silly thoughts, and he is somewhat uncomfortable about them. Furthermore, he is too old to be received into the army through regular channels. So his mother is forced to use her influence with Sir Joseph Mainwaring to secure her son a commission. Unfortunately, Basil does not distinguish himself with Sir Joseph. He goes instead to his sister's country estate to impede progress there. He blackmails the community by forcing the Connollies, obnoxious children evacuated from London, onto the unsuspecting villagers. Eventually Basil leaves the country, insinuates himself into an intelligence post, labels his friend Ambrose Silk a "fascist" and finally joins Peter Pastmaster's commando group.

Peter Pastmaster, the delightfully monstrous child of *Decline and Fall,* marries for dynastic reasons and in the process unexpectedly finds himself. Molly Meadows decides to marry him because he looks "like a little boy at his private school when his father has come to the sports in the wrong kind of a hat." [*Put Out More Flags*, 167] The fundamental innocence, surprisingly hidden under the roué's veneer, is here exposed. Alastair Trumpington, one-time lover of Margot Metroland, joins the army as a common soldier, not so much because he envies Peter Pastmaster his Sam Browne belt, but because he feels that he owes the world something. Sonia, his wife, says of him:

> You see he'd never done anything for the country and though we were always broke we had lots of money really and lots of fun. I believe he thought that perhaps if we hadn't had so much fun perhaps there wouldn't have been any war. Though how he could blame himself for Hitler I never quite saw . . . At least I do now in a way, . . . He went into the ranks as a kind of penance or whatever it is that religious people are always supposed to do. [*Put Out More Flags*, 114]

Here is Waugh tenuously moving into the penance prescribed by the Catholic Church, although his outlook in *Put Out More Flags* is specifically secular. But the introduction of the religious note indicates more strongly than ever before the direction he will take in *Brideshead Revisited*.

The dedication to the war allows Waugh to ring down the curtain on those characters that had peopled his world since *Decline and Fall*. Angela Lyne's husband, Cedric, goes to war and is killed, his death allowing Basil and Angela to culminate years of illicit relationship in marriage. Before his death Cedric comes to the conclusion that individual integrity is all that matters in the world:

> The great weapons of modern war did not count in single lives; it took a whole section to make a target

worth a burst of machine gun fire; a platoon or a motor
lorry to be worth a bomb. No one had anything against
the individual; as long as he was alone he was free and
safe; there's danger in numbers; divided we stand,
united we fall, thought Cedric, striding happily towards
the enemy, shaking from his boots all the frustrations
of corporate life. [*Put Out More Flags*, 220]

He had been thinking exactly what William Boot had
thought on retiring to the leisured life of Boot Magna.

With the marriage of Angela Lyne and Basil Seal, the
Bright Young People grow up and find in war a shadow of
that permanence whose lack Father Rothschild had, years
earlier, accurately diagnosed as the ill that made them hell-
bent for pleasure. Yet war is no solution, and Waugh is conscious of the fact.

Put Out More Flags lacks the spontaneity of *Decline and
Fall* and *Vile Bodies*, the ironic perspective of *A Handful of
Dust*. Occasionally it rises to the comic heights of its predecessors in its portrayal of the Connollies, the ordinary man's
version of Peter Pastmaster and Basil Seal. In *Put Out More
Flags* Waugh portrays the Bright Young People grown old.
Basil Seal's pranks, charming in a handsome rascal of twenty-
one, are tedious in an aging gasbag of thirty-eight. Not only
do the Bright Young People grow up, but they find it necessary to atone for what had before never been offenses. It is
Poppet Green, the surrealist artist, who prepares the stage
for the explicit religious statements of *Brideshead Revisited*:

> I wish I'd been to Church. I was brought up in a con-
> vent. I wanted to be a nun once. I wish I was a nun. I'm
> going to be killed. Oh, I wish I was a nun. Where's my
> gas mask? I shall go mad if I don't find my gas mask.
> [*Put Out More Flags*, 36]

Chapter 4

Roman Catholicism
and *Brideshead Revisited*

Those who had watched Waugh's progress were both pleased and outraged by the publication of *Brideshead Revisited* in 1945. Edmund Wilson, who had so admired the comic snobbery of *Decline and Fall* and *A Handful of Dust,* found a considerable falling off in Waugh's power although he readily admitted his lack of sympathy with the plight of the convert to Roman Catholicism:

> What happens when Evelyn Waugh abandons his comic convention—as fundamental to his previous art as that of any Restoration dramatist—turns out to be more or less disastrous. The writer in this more normal world, no longer knows his way: his deficiency in common sense here ceases to be an asset and gets him into some embarrassing situations, and his creative imagination, accustomed in his satirical fiction to work partly in two-dimensional caricature but now called upon for passion and motives, produces mere romantic fantasy. [Wilson, 299]

The basis of Wilson's earlier appreciation of Waugh had been the simple criterion that Waugh never apologized for or explained the actions of his characters. But Waugh, now writing within the demands of the traditional novel, was forced to explain not only the actions of his characters but also the philosophy which dominated their movements. It is quite true that there are romantic elements in the novel; but it is equally true that the romantic fantasy of the earlier sections makes up one of the most sensitive and most beautifully written portions of the book. To say, however, that *Brideshead Revisited* is "mere romantic fantasy" is to miss the theme of the novel. The element of fantasy enters strongly into the structure, but it is filtered through the personality of a hero who is incurably romantic.

The Catholic World, on the other hand, commented in terms quite opposite to those of Wilson. It found the work extremely interesting in the light of Waugh's development— the earlier novels had made a good many Catholics uncomfortable because of their unabashed malice and devastating wit. *The Catholic World* welcomed *Brideshead Revisited* as a work of art, but with modified rapture it commented on the Catholic bias from which the work was conceived:

> Make no mistake! The book is a work of art. No page, no paragraph should be passed by. Some have found it to be a sort of subtle apologia for "the good life" and even for Catholicism; but, if it is so intended, the author has drawn his lines so fine and shaded his colors so delicately that his purpose will remain hidden from all but keen eyes. In any event, he will meet with harsh criticisms among devout Catholics, loyal Oxonians, cultured members of the leisured class. Resentment will be awakened by his picture of Catholics clinging to outmoded traditions and assenting to unintelligent shibboleths, of wastrels and prodigals and incompetents of Oxford, of English gentry decadent, parasitical, ripe for liquidation.[17]

The Catholic World attempted to gloss over the criticism that the novel was flagrantly apologetic; but in maintaining the reverse, that if it were apologetic it was then subtly and indiscernibly so, the very important apologetic tone was minimized. And it is this aspect of apology which forms one of the novel's strongest points.

Brideshead Revisited is basically concerned with the influence of God on a Catholic English family. The book is divided into four sections: a short Prologue; a long section entitled "Et in Arcadia Ego"; a shorter section called "A Twitch upon the Thread"; and a short Epilogue. The plan is an ambitious one, and in length of time the novel spans the period between the two World Wars, the era of Eliot's *The Waste Land*. The Marchmains are a Catholic family living in a Protestant country, and their position is a peculiarly difficult one:

> The family history was typical of the Catholic squires of England; from Elizabeth's reign till Victoria's they lived sequestered lives, among their tenantry and kinsmen, sending their sons to school abroad, often marrying there, intermarrying, if not, with a score of families like themselves, debarred from all preferment, and learning in those lost generations, lessons which still could be read in the lives of the last three men of the house [Lady Marchmain's family]. [*Brideshead Revisited*, 123]

The reference made to Lady Marchmain's three brothers is important. For in their death—Lady Marchmain's brothers are killed in one way or another in the service of their country—Waugh symbolizes the decline of the British Catholic aristocracy.

To maintain their faith, the Marchmains must reconcile themselves to the idea of God compensating for lack of social benefits. Society, however, manages to exert its peculiar pressures on the individual members of the family so that three fall away from the Church. Lord Marchmain is converted to Roman Catholicism when he marries Theresa. She succeeds in bringing the Marchmains back to the religion of their ancestors, but he abandons her and his children when she comes to represent the inhibitions foisted on his personality by his adopted religion. He learns to hate her and all that is associated with her religion. Lord Marchmain lives in Italy with an Italian mistress; but he returns to die at Brideshead Castle, repentant for his turning away from the mercy of God and the consolations of his religion. Lady Marchmain not only represents the trammels of Roman Catholicism but she also points out an interesting aspect of Waugh's religion:

> When I was a girl we were comparatively poor, but still much richer than most of the world, and when I married I became very rich. It used to worry me, and I thought it wrong to have so many beautiful things when others had nothing. Now I understand that it is possible for the rich to sin by coveting the privileges of the poor. The poor have always been the favorites of God and his saints, but I believe that is one of the special achievements of grace to sanctify the whole of life, riches included. Wealth in pagan Rome was necessarily something cruel; it's not anymore. [*Brideshead Revisited,* 112]

Lady Marchmain gives voice to the idea that dominates the religious considerations of the novel. There is one set of principles for the rich and another for the poor. The poor are not "blessed" with the "curse" of wealth. With money goes the tradition and the gentleness and the goodness which Lady Marchmain considers her peculiar virtue and her particular grace. This is the same reliance on tradition and on the aristocracy that informed Waugh's earlier novels— in Brideshead Castle are symbolized the same ideas that were portrayed by Anchorage House and, to a far greater extent, by Hetton Abbey. But here these ideas are inextricably bound up with the tenets of Roman Catholicism. In

Lady Marchmain Waugh attempts to reconcile two attitudes which seem incompatible; and these same attitudes are apparent in the makeup of the hero of the novel, Charles Ryder.

Brideshead, the elder son of the family, compensates for not taking up a religious vocation by accepting the teachings and demands of his faith blindly, unquestionably, fanatically, while not understanding them at all. Sebastian Flyte, his brother, moves from the idyllic days of childhood, adolescence and youth into an adulthood of drunkenness and homosexuality. His mother comes to symbolize, as she does to his father, the unreasonable demands of Roman Catholicism. In her zeal to keep her son within the Church, she succeeds instead in alienating him from it and herself. Lady Marchmain and her Church, insisting on his spiritual and physical necessities, drive Sebastian to a life of debauchery; and the only meaning he can find in his unhappy existence is to care for Kurt, someone who needs him, someone he needs to care for.

Julia Flyte, finding it difficult to succeed in the world of Protestant English society because of her religion, falls in love with Rex Mottram, defies her mother, breaks away from the Church to marry in a Protestant ceremony, and eventually becomes the mistress of Charles Ryder. Cordelia, the youngest of the family, becomes the spokesman for the religious perplexities of her family. Even as a child she understands more deeply than anyone else the nature of the restraints imposed by her faith; and as a woman she explains to Charles Ryder the partiality of God for those who seek to evade His mercy:

> I wonder if you remember the story mummy read to us the evening Sebastian first got drunk—I mean the *bad* evening. "Father Brown" said something like "I caught him" (the thief) "with an unseen hook and an invisible line which is long enough to let him wander to the ends

of the world and still to bring him back with a twitch upon the thread." [*Brideshead Revisited*, 194–195]

Waugh's method is to trace the lives of the various individuals and to develop through them his theme of the divine purpose making itself apparent in the world of men. He is concerned primarily with the portraits of two members of this family, Sebastian and Julia Flyte, and with the influence of these two on the character of his hero, Charles Ryder.

Waugh's removal from the world of his creation, so apparent in the earlier novels, is considerably lessened in *Brideshead Revisited*. Indeed, to keep his action strictly within the definitions of Roman Catholicism and still consistent with his own personal attitudes, he seems at times to connive with his characters. Nevertheless he is prepared to accept and carry the standard of his religion, to apologize for it. Many of the attitudes that were discernible in the previous novels—the snobbery, the reliance on tradition, the exclusion of the workaday world—are apparent in *Brideshead;* but they are completely integrated into the theme. In tracing the workings of divine grace in the family of Sebastian and Julia, Waugh is forced to explain clearly his Roman Catholic bias. In choosing this theme—the mercy of the Roman Catholic God making itself apparent in the pagan world—he is forced to come down from the "altitude" that had characterized his position from *Decline and Fall* to *Put Out More Flags*. The irony, satire and comedy that had sustained these novels and made them comic masterpieces had also carried the weight of his snobbery and his dedication to the aristocracy. With the elimination of the satirical approach, Waugh had to devise another method of removing himself from the world of the Marchmains. He had to devise a method which would allow him to work with his delicate subject and yet afford him the distance necessary to manipulate his characters convincingly and according to the standards of the serious English novel. Yet he had to have a device which would allow him to make measured and cogent observations on the actions of the characters through whom he wished to portray the truth of his theme.

Faced with these problems, Waugh chose to represent his ideas through the views of Charles Ryder. All of his moral commentaries are filtered through the consciousness of the hero; and to understand Ryder is to understand Waugh's meaning. By using Ryder as a skeptical onlooker who becomes spiritually involved in the religious and social dilemma of the Catholic world of Brideshead, Waugh is able to trace his theme and make his moral commentary at the same time.

Charles Ryder serves then not only as the hero but also as the author's link with the real world. Charles is, in fact, the logical development of the innocent who so consistently figured in the earlier satirical pieces. But he has succeeded in growing out of the adolescent stage into the adult world. He loses a good deal on the way, his innocence included, but he gains something more valuable in the long run. The characterization of Ryder, his complete integration into the plot, his stumbling search for permanence, his self-realization, afford Waugh an excellent opportunity to display his skill at portraiture, something that had been lacking in his earlier work. Furthermore, the character develops as Charles learns more and more about the psychology of the Marchmains. His growth from a youthful romantic into a cynical adult and finally to a mature person capable of understanding love and the place of God in the world allows Waugh the opportunity to create the various moods of the period he portrays, moods distinguished by precision of utterance and beauty. It does not come as a surprise to the reader that Ryder is converted to Roman Catholicism by the novel's end. It is Waugh's subtlest point of artistic merit that he makes his hero, his observer, the one on whom the events of the narrative leave the imprint of faith. Charles's conversion is not explained in words; it is explained by the action of the novel as he moves towards a keener understanding of the family with which his life is inextricably bound.

Since it is through him that the reader sees the Flyte family, Charles's attitude of romanticism must be understood. The novel bears the subtitle, "The Sacred and Profane Memories of Captain Charles Ryder." The story is one of reminiscence, of nostalgia; and since it is so, Waugh is able to move from mood to mood to characterize his people and develop his theme. The second section of the book, which in actual length spans more than half the pages, deals with the period of youthful initiation. The section bears the title, "Et in Arcadia Ego." The scenes described are those of Charles's awakening into the world of youth, beauty and vitality. All that is fresh and appealing in life he associates with Sebastian Flyte. Through Sebastian's eyes, Charles discovers a world that had been completely closed to him. Reared by a father casual and generous in matters of money but niggardly in matters of affection, he holds the religious convictions his father had communicated to him—the heritage of the nineteenth century in which religion was a hobby, a matter of historical and literary interest. Ryder falls in love with Sebastian, as he does with the idea of youth, of spring, of romance itself. It is the Arcadian season come late upon him, and nothing can destroy the illusion. Charles is so much in love with his friend's innocence that nothing can persuade him of the potential dangers of Sebastian's charms, for Sebastian is much more than the object of Ryder's affection —he is in a very real sense his other self. And Charles comes to think and feel much as Sebastian does. This affection is correctly analyzed by Cara, Lord Marchmain's mistress, when she says, "It is a kind of love that comes to children before they know its meaning. In England it comes to you when you are almost men; I think I like that. It is better to have that kind of love for another boy than for a girl."

[*Brideshead Revisited,* 90–91] In Theresa Marchmain, Cara's lover had seen the betrayal of his boyhood—innocence, God, hope. Lady Marchmain had done nothing to deserve his hate but to be loved by a boy who had not grown up.

Sebastian, too, is in love with the idea of childhood, of innocence and its beauty. But in this love there is an implicit refusal to grow up. What he admires in Charles is not only a reciprocal innocence and appreciation of beauty but also an ability to choose, the capacity for reckoning the consequences of choice. In other words, Sebastian admires Charles's independence, his spiritual freedom.

Ryder, then, exists in Sebastian's youth; they share a fundamental innocence. Still there is a part of Sebastian's life that Charles cannot understand—his religion. As he becomes more and more intimate with the Marchmains, Ryder begins to appreciate the influence of Catholicism on the life of his friend. At first Sebastian had feared to allow Charles to meet his family, lest he become their ally against him. When Lady Marchmain fails to make Charles adapt himself to her demands, she removes Sebastian from him and his influence. In her zeal, Lady Marchmain attempts to force religion on her son but succeeds, instead, in completely demoralizing him. Her insistence on this issue confirms his drunkenness and loses him to the world.

Sebastian does not drink to recapture the happiness of his childhood, however. Rather he drinks for the same reason that his father keeps Cara as his mistress—to protect himself from happiness. For if he accepts happiness, Sebastian must accept God and responsibility. But he cannot be forced into this acceptance as his mother insists. His debauchery becomes his method of shutting out the demands of his conscience. He comes very near to damnation, but he is rescued because, as Cordelia says, "He is very near to God." [*Brideshead Revisited,* 270] Without a religious vocation herself, Cordelia finds comfort in her brother's holy end, a drunkard and a penitent, in a monastery in Carthage. She finds comfort in the thought that he finally succumbs to a religious vocation against which he had struggled most of his unhappy life. Sebastian had seen and felt the presence of innocence in the world; and in his youthful way he had thought to save the happiness, refusing to accept until the very end its source, God.

It is Cordelia, again, who makes the commentary that fixes the portrait of Lady Marchmain:

> Well, you see, she was saintly but she wasn't a saint. No one could really hate a saint, could they. They can't really hate God either. When they want to hate Him and His saints they have to find something like them- selves and pretend it's God and hate that. [*Brideshead Revisited*, 195]

Men may hate Theresa Marchmain but God loves her. Lady Marchmain has little in common with Lady Anchorage.

With the loss of Sebastian's youthful innocence, Ryder's Arcadian period ends. He leaves behind youth, adolescence, romance, illusion. "Henceforth," he says, "I live in a world of three dimensions—with the aid of my five senses." [*Brideshead Revisited*, 150] He turns a page in his own book.

The love that Charles had felt for Sebastian is, in fact, a forerunner of his love for Julia. On their first meeting Charles remarked that she so resembled Sebastian that, sitting beside her, he had been confused by the double illusion of famili- arity and strangeness. Married outside the Church to Rex Mottram, Julia had discovered early in her marriage that the man for whom she had given up her religion was "a tiny bit of a man pretending he was the whole." [*Brideshead Re- visited*, 177] She falls in love with Ryder, and in her love for him she compounds the sin that she lives in already as Mottram's wife. In her union with Charles she finds a shade of permanence (the same permanence that the Bright Young

People had been seeking), and she plans to insure this by marriage. To marry Charles, Julia must divorce her husband as Charles must divorce his wife, whom he has no reason or obligation to love since discovering she had committed adultery. At first Julia refuses to accept the fact that, according to the tenets of her religion, she is living in sin and that all possibility of redemption is lost to her as long as she continues in the state of sin. To her, her sin is the betrayal of God, the nails which she feels she herself has driven into the body of Christ, the betrayal that casts man into the waste land:

> Mummy dying with it; Christ dying with it, nailed hand and foot; hanging over the bed in the night nursery; hanging year after year in the dark little study at Farm Street with the shining oil-cloth; hanging in the dark church where only the old charwoman raises the dust and one candle burns; hanging at noon, high among the crowds and soldiers; no comfort except a sponge of vinegar and the kind words of a thief. . . .
> Never the shelter of the caves or the castle walls. Outcast in the desolate places where the hyenas roam at night and the rubbish heaps smoke in the daylight. No way back; the gates barred; all the saints and angels posted along the walls. Nothing but bare stones and dust and the smouldering dumps. Thrown away, scrapped, rotting down; the old man with lupus and the forked stick limps out at nightfall to turn the rubbish, hoping for something to put in his sack, something marketable, turns away in disgust. [*Brideshead Revisited*, 252–253]

The thread twitches for Julia; it has already twitched for Sebastian; and now it must twitch for their father.

When Lord Marchmain returns to Brideshead Castle to die, his family thinks about a priest to help prepare him for death. When Father McKay arrives, Lord Marchmain sends him away. Furious at the intrusion on his privacy, the old man explains to the priest in haughty language that he has not been a practitioner of his wife's religion for over twenty-five years and that he feels no need of the comforts of her Church. But Lord Marchmain fears death, and in the end the twitching thread pulls him back into the fold.

At first indignant at the insistence of the family that the invalid see a priest, Charles unaccountably finds himself praying that the old man will die repentant. At the moment of the old man's capitulation, Charles realizes what he has long suspected, that he and Julia can never marry. He learns that the demands of the conscience are too strong to be denied, that only in accepting the mercy of God can happiness be found in life. Charles accepts the fact that his love for Julia is the forerunner of a greater love, as his love for Sebastian had been a forerunner of his love for Julia. He had never ceased to love Sebastian, for he had loved him in Julia; and in Sebastian he had loved her. In his love for the two of them is implicit a love of God:

> . . . perhaps all our loves are merely hints and symbols; vagabond language scrawled on gate posts and paving along the weary road that others have tramped before us. . . . [*Brideshead Revised,* 265]

The love of Charles for Julia is the "shadow which turns the corner always a pace or two ahead of us." [*Brideshead Revisited,* 265] And this is the explanation of Charles's conversion which at first strikes the reader as unconvincing. He had learned to see and feel with Sebastian; through him he had learned to love Julia. Both loves presage a love of God. And in the love of God he discovers permanence, or rather he falls into that shadow of permanence which turns the corner always a pace or two ahead of him.

From the traditions of the past had sprung Brideshead Castle. The chapel had been grafted onto the house by

Theresa Marchmain, but the graft revitalized the old branch by returning to it the springs of love from which it had originally grown. Out of unhappiness and decadence the grace of God had shown itself to be unflagging and persistent in showing the way to that permanece that all the Marchmains seek. From their peace Charles Ryder derives a peace of his own; from the tragedy in which he had been an important player, he gains something that he had never thought possible. He discovers his own grail—hope.

Brideshead Revisited reveals the complete maturity of Evelyn Waugh as an artist. The novel is brilliantly conceived and brilliantly executed. The integration of plot, character and action with the theme denotes the most competent artistry. It is wrong, I think, to condemn the novel as flagrantly romantic, as Edmund Wilson does; or to insist that romantic adolescence is "Waugh's only touchstone of significance for human existence" and therefore inadequate, as D. S. Savage does. To do either is to miss the meaning. *Brideshead Revisited* essentially portrays a real experience of life. But it does much more than this: it is a considered and mature evaluation of the place of religion in the modern world. It is true that there are elements which at times intrude—Waugh's snobbery and his preoccupation with the aristocracy make themselves uncomfortably apparent. But the impression the novel makes is a universal and valid one because it does deal with the real world convincingly. The earlier novels had been caricatures and distortions of reality; they constituted his apprenticeship. *A Handful of Dust* had prepared the way for the discussion of the marital problem; and it had indicated the possibility of finding a way out of the waste land through the doors of the Church. *Brideshead Revisited* indicates strongly that belief in God is the most logical answer to contemporary problems. The pattern of conversion that the hero falls into is similar to Eliot's own as he moves from *The Waste Land* into the repentance of

Ash Wednesday and slowly into the more cadenced harmonies of the *Four Quartets*.

Brideshead Revisited is, furthermore, an apology for Waugh's faith. To deny this is to deny one of the strengths of the novel. In the experience of life which the narrative creates, the God of salvation is the God of the Roman Catholic Church. The influence of this Church on the lives of the characters is astonishingly pervasive and, in the long run, astonishingly effective. There are many kinds of religious conversion—Waugh pictures one that takes place within the Roman Church. This he does in all likelihood because he is himself a Catholic. In the Church he finds strength and tradition—permanence; in it he finds reasoned logic, an avenue to salvation. But the universal validity of his message is undeniable. For he insists that God is merciful, that His grace cannot be denied. He insists on the place of God in the real and the living world. The problem is not that he writes about Catholics; the problem is that he writes about Catholics for a predominantly Protestant audience. If at times he seems uncomfortable in the manipulation of his theme, it is because he feels the weight of his task.

Perhaps the signal triumph of the novel is the language in which it is written. *Brideshead Revisited* succeeds in re-creating an age. It moves from sheer romanticism, from pastoral and idyllic beauty, to worldly cynicism, to mellowed retrospection in language so commensurate with the moods that one is convinced of the authenticity of the portrayal by sheer force of the words themselves. In *Brideshead Revisited* Evelyn Waugh proves himself a master of the English tongue; for his style, characterized by an austere simplicity and an aptness as well as cadence of phrase, succeeds in sustaining and even enhancing the religious theme.

Chapter 5

Towards *Helena*
and Church History

Between *Brideshead Revisited* and *Helena* (1950), the next novel to take up the religious theme, appeared *Scott-King's Modern Europe* (1947) and *The Loved One* (1948). *The Loved One* grew out of observations made by Waugh while visiting Forest Lawn Memorial Park in California. The novel is not only an ironic portrait of a streamlined funeral parlor, but it is also a bitter and caustic condemnation of the American way of life.

For *Life* magazine Waugh wrote an article which appeared in the issue of September 29, 1947. He described the acres of reclaimed California desert which house Forest Lawn, and he discussed the various benefits derived from burial in the park:

> The body does not decay; it lives more chic in death than ever before, in its indestructible Class A steel-and-concrete shelf; the soul goes straight from the Slumber Room to Paradise, where it enjoys an endless infancy. . . .[18]

Waugh studied the American attitude toward death as symbolized by the cemetery, and he found implicit in it an elimination of the traditional concepts of heaven and hell. The emphasis, he discovered, was put not on the dignity of

Catholic, the fact of death is not to be feared at all: he is solaced with the fantasy of another world in which everyone who has died in the flesh is somehow supposed to be still alive and in which it is supposed to be possible to help souls advance themselves by buying candles to burn in churches. [Wilson, 304–305]

Scott-King's Modern Europe, published in book form in 1949, appeared first in *Cosmopolitan* magazine under the title, *A Sojourn in Neutralia.* Like *The Loved One* it is more a novelette than a novel. It exhibits a return to Waugh's earlier satirical method, but it lacks the spontaneity and the gusto of the earlier books. It develops ironically Scott-King's position in the Mediterranean state of Neutralia, but it misses its mark because the situations are neither comic enough nor distorted enough to make the irony pointed.

The novel retells the adventures of a middle-aged Classics master at an English boys' school who is invited to help in the tercentenary celebration in honor of a dimly-known poet —Bellorious. Scott-King accepts the invitation, and in Bellacita, the capital, he somehow manages to disgrace himself with his "fellow travelers" and is labelled a fascist sympathizer. The government-host immediately relinquishes all responsibility for him once the celebration is ended, and Scott-King, dressed as an Ursuline nun, returns to England via an underground that leads through the Holy Land. The result of his adventure is to confirm his belief that there is little hope for the world and that there is nothing that he can do to equip youth to live in chaos: "I think it would be very wicked indeed to do anything to fit a boy for the modern world," he says to the headmaster when he is asked to teach a more practical subject such as history, preferably economic history.[20] By insisting on the Classics, Scott-King takes what he considers the longest possible view under the circumstances.

The most interesting aspect of the work is the reappearance of the innocent. Scott-King, like William Boot of *Scoop*, retires happily into obscurity, content to let the world go round without him. *Scott-King's Modern Europe* is a far different kind of novel from Waugh's next, *Helena*.

Helena appeared in 1950. In the Preface Waugh tells his reader that his primary aim is to retell an old story, to set straight certain confusions concerning the Church of which he is a member:

> It is reported (and I, for one, believe it) that some few years ago a lady prominent for her hostility to the Church returned from a visit to Palestine in a state of exaltation. "I got the real low-down at last," she told her friends. "The whole story of the crucifixion was made up by a British woman named Ellen. Why, the guide showed me the very place where it happened. Even the priests admit it. They call the place 'the Invention of the Cross.'" [21]

Waugh insists, however, that the purpose of the novel is only incidentally an apologetic one, that his primary concern is with the Empress Helena, the mother of Constantine the Great. Although he is loud in his insistence, the most interesting aspects of the novel are those which are apologetic in nature. For as a novel *Helena* is not completely successful. The novel that should deal with the character of the heroine deals more convincingly with the era in which she lived. There is an indication, too, that Waugh is drawing a parallel with modern times. Helena's search for the City is, indeed, the timeless search for God.

Waugh allows himself the novelist's privilege in the reconstruction of his heroine's life. He whimsically makes her the daughter of the Old King Cole of the nursery rhymes, deviates from history by establishing the place of her birth at Colchester rather than York, and ingeniously introduces the figure of the Wandering Jew into the narrative. Since

Waugh insists that *Helena* is a novel, the reader is perfectly willing to accept the novelist's inventions.

The period of Helena's youth is described with that peculiar insight and brilliance Waugh reserves for depicting youth. The young Helena is portrayed as a sensitive, intelligent, red-haired English girl whose chief delights are those of the outdoors. The curiosity which at the end of her life finds its fulfillment in the discovery of the Cross is seen in her early youth. "When I am educated," she says to her slave Marcias, "I shall go and find the real Troy—Helen's." [*Helena*, 5]. And again she says, "I'm going to see everything for myself one day, when I'm educated." [*Helena*, 6] The City is, indeed, the city of God, the city that Tony Last had struggled towards but never reached.

Helena lives in the world of the *Iliad* and the *Odyssey*. She sees herself as Helen of Troy with white arms and tender sentiments, and she dreams of the love of Paris for Helen. Her favorite daydream is riding horses, fearlessly and masterfully. Through her tutor Marcias she learns to have an immense respect for Longinus, and he becomes for her a second heroic myth. Into this world of romantic dreams comes Constantius Chlorus; and he offers a more definite pattern to her dream of far-off places—Rome, The City. They marry and move into the world of politics and intrigue, for Chlorus is of the Imperial family and likely to become Emperor. What impresses Helena most on their marriage journey to the Danube is the wall that Rome has thrown around the world. To Chlorus it represents permanence and stability; but to Helena it is the limits of man's progress and she wonders if there is anything beyond it. She wonders if The City might not some day break out: "Couldn't the wall be at the limits of the world and all men, civilized and barbarian, have a share in The City?" [*Helena*, 49] Hers is the missionary's dream, the vision of the evangelist, the saint.

With her gradual awareness of the place of woman in

marriage, Helena's youthful ardor fades. And the murder of Longinus shatters the last of her heroic dreams. The desire to see Rome, The City, leaves the girl, to be replaced by the curiosity of the woman. For Helena constantly seeks to understand the meaning behind the mystery of things. In a matter-of-fact way she seeks matter-of-fact answers to straightforward questions. Constantius Chlorus leaves her for a mistress he eventually murders. He takes to religion and attempts to explain to Helena the origin of the world as taught by the cult of Mithras. She listens attentively to the beautiful tale, and then she asks the straight question which had always confounded her tutor:

> And when did this happen? How do you know, if no one was there? And if the bull was the first thought of Ormazd and he had to be killed in order to make the earth, why didn't Ormazd just think of the earth straight away? And if the earth is evil, why did Mithras kill the bull at all? . . . What I want to know is, do you really believe all this? Believe, I mean, that Mithras killed his bull in the same way you believe Uncle Claudius beat the Goths? [*Helena*, 97]

She asks the same questions of Lactantius, a refugee Christian to whom she offers shelter; and from him she learns something of the beliefs of the Christians. She learns that Christ the Son of God was made man to atone for the sins of men, His teachings set down by His followers, and His memory preserved in the lore of the Church. Nevertheless, she cannot accept these teachings, even when she learns that her son, Constantine, has won his signal battle under the sign of the Cross. Helena has the will to believe; but she lacks grace, the virtue necessary to confirm belief. Somehow, sometime, she receives this grace, for she is baptized. Whether she merely conformed to the prevailing fashion or became a brimming vehicle of grace is not known. "She was a seed in a vast germination." [*Helena*, 140]

The curious and imaginative girl who married Constantius Chlorus is transformed in her old age into a staunch and formidable member of her Church. Inspired by divine grace, she goes first to Rome, the city that had held her youthful dreams, to discover that it is not The City. There she is reunited with Constantine, who had conquered under the banner of her God. From Rome she goes to the Holy Land, seeking there concrete proof of the ministry of her God on earth—the Cross:

> I bet He's just waiting to have one of us to go find it—just at this moment when it's most needed. Just at this moment when everyone is forgetting it and chattering about the hypostatic union, there's a solid chunk of wood waiting for them to have their silly heads knocked against. [*Helena*, 209]

Philosophers and antiquaries quail before the sharpness of her perceptions. At Easter time, in an opium-induced dream, Helena sees a Jew, an incense merchant, one who, because he had reproved the dying God for loitering on his doorstep, is made to live perpetually; he is the Wandering Jew of legend. From him Helena learns the fate of the True Cross. She sees in her dream the carnival that will be made of religion should her discovery be given to the world. She remains firm in her conviction that the will of God will predominate over the shortcomings of man. In her discovery of the True Cross she accomplishes what she had dreamed of doing as a girl—she finds her own Troy. She succeeds in doing what only saints are capable of doing—she conforms completely to the will of God. "That was the particular, humble purpose for which she had been created." [*Helena*, 260] The divine grace that had induced her to become a Christian does not desert her; and the Empress Helena recaptures the romance and the idealism of her youth—all questions answered.

This briefly is the legend of the life of Saint Helena. It shows the workings of divine grace in an individual, but it is the least interesting aspect of the novel.

In tracing the divine purpose in the fourth century after Christ, Waugh must necessarily deal, and deal authentically, with the historical aspects of Constantine the Great's reign. His portrayal of Constantine, the weak and decadent ruler of the world, is the portrait of an era. This is the age in which the Christian ideology came into its own. Constantine is not shown as the pious and saintly ruler who saw a sign in the heavens and went into battle at the Milvian bridge and conquered under that sign. He is pictured, first of all, as the shrewd and practical man of affairs who recognized the political expediency of adopting openly an ideology which it would have been dangerous to refute. He made terms with an ally of unknown strength, the Christians. He tolerated the Christian ideology when it was tactically the thing to do. By granting amnesty, he not only relieved the Christians of the "privilege" of martyrdom but also assured his own position on the throne. He did not fight for God and Christianity; he fought for himself. His son Crispus says, "It makes you feel such an ass being told afterwards that you were fighting for religion." [*Helena,* 163] To escape the fate of his predecessors, Constantine made an effective ally of a force that could have destroyed him. But by doing so, he opened the way to that peace and prosperity to which recorded history testifies. Constantine not only secured his own poistion but unwittingly became the tool of God, the vehicle of His divine will.

As a man Constantine remains outside the Church proper. He refuses to be baptized, though his mother pleads with him to do so. He wishes to save that last refuge of the new religion until the end. Here Waugh develops another aspect of his Roman Catholicism: the belief that baptism washes all sins away automatically. Denying his conscience, Constantine removes himself from grace; and grace is essential to salvation. He mistakenly relies on a last minute repentance which may or may not be accorded him. Constantine grants religious freedom to others, and he himself lives according to the barbaric creed of those emperors whose descendant he is. He has no qualms about murdering his father-in-law, his brother-in-law, or his wife, Fausta. Here is again manifested a pagan attitude toward death. Murder is an expedient, not a sin. Constantine allows Fausta to lead him to the murder of Crispus, his son; and he rationalizes this action by telling himself that the great must be ruthless to preserve their greatness. He succeeds in vulgarizing the standard under which he achieved his victory at the Milvian bridge. The Cross is made into a labarum, a gorgeously wrought standard upon which all his exploits—those before and those after the battle of the Milvian bridge—are recorded. Helena recognizes the absurdity of this and remonstrates with him; but Constantine is adamant. He continues to consider himself the chosen of God though he remains outside the Church. His conscience makes itself apparent in his black moods, and in one of these he sees Fausta as the incarnation of that evil which tempts him from goodness. As a matter of course he has her roasted alive in her bath.

Constantine is, in essence, Waugh's portrait of power without grace. The influence of Rome was on the wane when Constantine became Emperor. By uniting himself with a power force—for Christianity was that—Constantine succeeded in reinvesting a new dignity and a new meaning in the name "Rome."

These are the apologetic notes of the novel. The portrait of Helena serves merely as an excuse for Waugh to portray his theme of divine grace making itself apparent in the real world despite the pettiness and absurdities of men. In *Helena*, as in *Brideshead Revisited*, order is brought out of chaos, and faith is established where none had been before.

From out of the decadence of the court of Constantine, truth comes, and this same truth is concretely manifested to Helena in the wood of the True Cross. In the end Christianity proves its essential validity: it becomes the electrifying force that sustains the world.

Helena is not successful as a novel. Even the strength of the prose style is not enough to sustain an often flagging narrative. Taking pains to insist that he is writing a novel, though it is based as nearly as possible on authentic history, Waugh instead defines a time and apologizes for his religion while doing so. He does not succeed in integrating his materials. As a picture of a saint's life, however, the work is more successful. For Waugh succeeds admirably in depicting a cantankerous, crotchety old woman who becomes a brimming vehicle of divine grace.

As a girl Helena is delightfully charming; as an old woman she is convincingly saintly—if saintliness comprises fanaticism. Since he accepts the license of the novelist, Waugh is perfectly within his rights to take privileges with history, though he claims to take few. If as a novelist he can accord his heroine a dream in which she is told by the Wandering Jew where to dig for the True Cross, why can he not describe the moment of his saint's conversion? Instead he relies on the privilege of the historian—there are no documented records of Helena's baptism; therefore there is no need to describe it. He misses a very important point of psychological interest by glibly avoiding the issue. A few pages before, he had told his reader that Helena was too old to consider changing from the religion of her ancestors. In *Brideshead Revisited* it had not been necessary to describe the actual moment of Charles Ryder's conversion, though Waugh had done so subtly, meaningfully. In *Helena*, however, he asks his reader to accept the fact that an intellectually curious young girl develops into a middle-aged woman who seeks a meaning to the riddle of life and through the grace of God is allowed to find religious conviction as well as the wood of the True Cross. These points are not consistent within the portrayal of her character.

Helena is more valid as an historical commentary and as an apology for Roman Catholicism than as a novel which creates an experience of life. The religious theme is, of course, the controlling one; but it does not sustain the characterization or the plot incidents. Individual scenes are sharply drawn—Fausta's murder, Constantine's sermon—but the elements of the novel remain disparate. The theology underlying the structure is too apparent—too dogmatic, if possible. The religious theme fights for prominence, and it achieves it at the expense of art.

Chapter 6

Waugh at Arms

In *Men at Arms* (1952) Waugh fuses the comic convention of *Decline and Fall* with the serious religious considerations of *Brideshead Revisited*. *Men at Arms* was the first novel of a planned trilogy dealing with the years of the Second World War. And the strides that Waugh has made can be easily discerned by comparing the novel to *Put Out More Flags,* which also dealt with the early months of the war. In *Men at Arms* there is a greater comprehension of issues and men. The earlier novel seems a child's toy by comparison. Although the satirical elements of the earlier books are present, Waugh in *Men at Arms* demonstrates a great awareness of the real world; and he makes a serious commentary on it through the medium of the comic spirit. His removal from the world of his invention, so apparent in *Vile Bodies* and *Black Mischief,* had been maintained in lesser degree through the character of the narrator in *Brideshead Revisited*. In *Men at Arms* he deals directly with the subject. And the return to the comic convention does not denote any falling off in power. Rather the synthesis of the comic and the serious succeeds in raising the novel above the level of amusing farce to that of tragi-comedy. There is some of the hard, sharp metal of Shakespeare's *Measure for Measure* and *The Tempest* in the novel. It succeeds because Waugh achieves a delicate balance between the elements of the comic and the serious and shows himself fully aware of the purgative value of the comic spirit. The irony of which he is master lends perspective to the religious theme.

The satire of *Men at Arms* is not the malicious cut and jab of *Decline and Fall*. It is mellow, reflective; the raillery is gentle; and the situations are funny in themselves, whereas before they depended on cruelty and malice for their humor. What William York Tindall termed Waugh's "monkish loathing" is replaced by a whimsical, benevolent view of the world and of man. Waugh even models one of his characters, Ben Ritchie-Hook, from the pages of *Peter Pan*. Guy Crouchback, the hero, is assuredly in love with the army. And the satire which Waugh directs at that institution is the lover's gentle remonstrance. It is a far cry from the iron-fisted attacks on boys' schools and British prisons of *Decline and Fall*. The youthful extravagance is gone, replaced by a mature appraisal of the ridiculous. There are scenes in the novel that are among the funniest Waugh has written. And what distinguishes them is the considered perspective of the novelist, the understanding and tolerant attitude. It is as though Waugh has come down from the summit and identified himself as one of men.

The satire is directed chiefly at the army. The routine is brilliantly described as are the soldiers who comprise the regiment. The title of the book, *Men at Arms*, indicates the importance of these men to the action; and Guy Crouchback, the hero, is but a soldier among them. Indeed, Waugh characterizes Crouchback's beloved regiment through the Leonards and the Sarum-Smiths, the Hayters and the Tickeridges. Perhaps the most important of these men at arms is Apthorpe, Waugh's contribution to an imposing gallery of braggart soldiers. Three-fourths of the novel is a record of Apthorpe's rise to prominence. He begins as Apthorpe's "gloriosus," then becomes "furibundus" when the Brigadier appropriates his thunder box. The last section of the novel is entitled "Apthorpe Immolatus," and there is a suggestion that Apthorpe is sacrificed for some destiny higher than the war. The war, then, is seen through the various men who shoulder arms. And they are far removed from Peter Pastmaster, Alastair Trumpington, and Basil Seal. They are real men; and Waugh could not have created either them or the experience of life within which they figure had he not first grappled with the portraits of Theresa Marchmain and Charles Ryder.

It must be emphasized that Waugh could not have written *Men at Arms* had he not first of all oriented his religious bias in *Brideshead Revisited*. There is a great deal of absurdity in the portrayal of Crouchback, but the absurdity is Waugh's touchstone to the core of meaning that distinguishes the actions of the character. And Crouchback's Roman Catholicism helps make him the strongest of Waugh's male portraits.

In Guy Crouchback Waugh introduces again the character of the innocent, but the uncomprehending naiveté of a Paul Pennyfeather is replaced by a sense of the inadequacy of modern man in the confusion of the modern world. Through his hero Waugh defines the anatomy of innocence. And Crouchback's Roman Catholicism not only sustains the characterization but also directs the action of the plot. As in *Brideshead Revisited* and *Helena* the theme is that of the divine purpose making itself apparent in the phenomenal world. The element of apology, however, is gone. For Waugh seems at ease with his materials. His comic sense restores the balance that seemed to have deserted the novels since *Brideshead Revisited*. In *Men at Arms* Waugh is concerned with stony, theological issues, but now more than ever before they are integrated into the pattern of the novel.

Guy Crouchback leaves his Italian home to enlist in the English army at the outbreak of the Second World War. Like Alastair Trumpington and Peter Pastmaster, Guy seeks revitalization in his dedication to the English cause. Eight

years before the story begins Guy had been divorced by his
wife, Virginia. Since that time he has lived a spiritual cripple.
For Guy is a Roman Catholic whose church will not permit
him to remarry—and he is the last of the Crouchbacks. He
has prosecuted several sordid love affairs, but they have only
succeeded in making him feel his spiritual inadequacies more
keenly. It never occurs to him to remarry in order to procure
an heir, even though his family name dies with him. Roman
Catholicism has been his family's mainstay since the time
of Henry II; and Guy cannot, would not, go against the
teachings of his Church. God cannot be served in dishonor.
Through the Crouchbacks Waugh again points out his concern with the traditions of the Catholic aristocracy in England, the same concern that preoccupied him in earlier
novels. The Crouchback estate has declined since the time of
Henry I, and all that remains is the house at Broome. Guy's
father does not sell the house; he lets it instead to a convent:
"And the sanctuary lamp still burned at Broome as of old." [22]
The religious traditions of the family are symbolized in Guy's
father, and they are manifested in Guy.

Guy knows that he is not *simpatico*. Despite the fact that
he is of their religion and speaks their tongue fluently, though
without expression, Guy is not popular with his Italian
neighbors. For in typical Italian fashion the natives around
Santa Dulcina delle Rocce prefer the flamboyant and the
picturesque. Guy, however, understands; his lack of popu-
larity is another aspect of that inadequacy that sets him
apart from the rest of the world. In the popular saint of the
village, "il Santo Inglese," he sees a counterpart to himself.
Roger of Waybroke, after padlocking his wife, had left England to fight the holy war. He had fallen, ridiculously, in a
local dispute between two minor Italian nobles:

> . . . the people of Santa Dulcina delle Rocce, to whom
> the supernatural order in all its ramifications was ever
> present and ever more lively than the humdrum world

about them, adopted Sir Roger and despite all clerical
remonstrance canonized him, brought him their troubles
and touched his sword for luck, so that its edge was
always bright. [*Men at Arms*, 6–7]

To the effigy of "il Santo Inglese" Guy goes; and he runs his
finger, as the fishermen of the village do, along the knight's
sword. "Sir Roger, pray for me," he says, "and for our endan-
gered kingdom." [*Men at Arms*, 7] Guy who had suffered "a
tiny stroke of paralysis," his physical faculties "just percep-
tibly impaired," goes to England to take up his sword against
the Infidel. He goes off to fight for God and country.

Guy is made of the same idealistic stuff as his predecessors; he is romantic. Like Charles Ryder and like Tony
Last he lives in the world of the nursery and the schoolroom.
He finds an opportunity to give new meaning to his life by
rallying to the aid of his country. He bridles against a priest
who delivers a sermon, from the pulpit, that does not coin-
cide with the romantic notions of grandeur which are to
him the essence of heroism:

> The priest was a recent graduate from Maynooth who
> had little enthusiasm for the Allied cause or for the
> English army, which he regarded merely as a provoca-
> tion to immorality in the town. His sermon that morning
> was not positively offensive; there was nothing in it to
> make the basis of a complaint; but when he spoke of
> "this terrible time of doubt, danger and suffering in
> which we live," Guy stiffened. It was a time of glory and
> dedication. [*Men at Arms*, 69]

In his enthusiasm for his Halberdiers, Guy discovers, as
Charles Ryder had discovered in his affection for Sebastian,
a lost period of his youth: "It seemed to Guy that in the last
weeks he had been experiencing something he had missed in
his boyhood, a happy adolescence." [*Men at Arms*, 50] He
is older than the other members of his officer training group

and is respectfully called "Uncle" because of his seniority.
For the first time in his life he feels that he belongs to the
world of men. He feels a member of that society that he
has always been apart from. He grows a moustache and
adopts a monocle, to make surer his orientation into this new
and delightful world. But, as he suspects, he is running
away from himself.

The youthful idyll is enhanced by the friendships of
barracks life. Guy feels a sense of camaraderie which he has
not known since his days in the nursery. He makes a friend
of Apthorpe, the other middle-aged man in the unit; and
in Apthorpe he discovers the element of schoolboy horseplay
that he has never known. Apthorpe keeps a thunder-box with
his gear. The thunder-box is a chemically operated field
latrine. The Brigadier, Ben Ritchie-Hook, learns of the
thunder-box and appropriates it for his own use by declaring
the shed that Apthorpe stores it in off limits to all below the
rank of Brigadier. A battle ensues; at times it seems that
Ritchie-Hook will be victorious, at others, Apthorpe. The
final laurel goes to the Brigadier, however, for he dispossesses
Apthorpe by turning the thunder-box into a booby trap that
explodes just as Apthorpe is about to claim his rights of
property. When Guy takes a hand in the battle, the reader
realizes that this is the schoolboy horseplay he has missed, as
Apthorpe is the "chum" he had failed to meet. This interpre-
tation seems inevitable, for even the setting of the novel,
Kut-al-Imara house, is a converted boys' school.

The mock battle is, in fact, the preparation for the African
adventure with Ritchie-Hook. Guy is chosen to lead, unoffi-
cially, a reconnaissance patrol into an African beach. The
Brigadier goes along as supernumerary, unknown to Guy
who is in command of the detail. The mission is the culmina-
tion of boyhood dreams of high adventure:

"... I've chosen your squadron for the task Truslove."
"Thank you, sir. What are our chances of getting

through?" "It can be done, Truslove, or I shouldn't be
sending you. If anyone can do it, you can. And I can tell
you this, my boy, I'd give all my seniority and all those
bits of ribbon on my chest to be with you. But my duty
lies here with the regiment. Good luck to you, my boy.
You'll need it." . . . The words, came back to him from
a summer Sunday evening at his preparatory school, in
the headmaster's drawing-room, the three top forms sitting on the floor, some in a dream of home, others, Guy
among them—spell-bound. [*Men at Arms*, 208]

Ritchie-Hook succeeds in bringing back a souvenir of the
adventure—the bloody head of a Negro soldier. Here the
macabre of *Black Mischief* reappears, but it is more ironical
than comic, as it had been in the early novel. Ritchie-Hook's
unauthorized prank has serious repercussions for Guy; he is
held officially responsible for the General's "invasion" of
Africa. At the novel's end he is sent back to England with
Ritchie-Hook to answer the questions of their military
superiors. Before he leaves, Guy makes a visit to Apthorpe
who is in hospital. He takes Apthorpe a bottle of whiskey at
his superior's suggestion; and this bottle hastens his friend's
death. For Apthorpe drinks the liquor all at once, and, in
his weakened condition, the strain is too great. But Guy
knows that these mishaps will leave no scars; for his innocence remains unimpaired:

> His fingers shook but it was nerves not conscience
> which troubled him; he was familiar with shame; this
> trembling, hopeless sense of disaster was something of
> quite another order; something that would pass and
> leave no mark. [*Men at Arms*, 310]

These, he understands, are the ways of the world, not the
ways of God. Guy has not sinned according to the precepts
of his church, and he knows that what has happened is in

no way connected with the state of his soul. He has in no way consciously willed these disasters.

From Mr. Goodall, a student of heraldry fascinated by the history of the Catholic aristocracy in England, Guy, while still in training for his officer's pips, learns the story of an English Catholic who had been divorced by his wife. They had met later and between them had produced a child. In the eyes of the Church, Goodall tells Guy, there was no sin; for these two were still married, the Church not recognizing divorce. The child produced by this union, though it bore the name of the woman's legal husband, preserved a great family from extinction, although under another and an uninteresting name. This was the working of divine providence, Goodall insists. Guy is much interested in the account, for Virginia has recently been much in his thoughts. "Mr. Goodall," he asks, "do you believe that God's providence concerns itself with the perpetuation of the English aristocracy?" To which Goodall answers, "But, of course. And with sparrows, too, we are taught." [*Men at Arms*, 147] At his first opportunity Guy goes to London to see his wife.

When Virginia first sees him, she comments on the moustache. To please her he has it shaved off; and when he sees his old self in the mirror, he realizes that for many weeks he has been playing a part, for he cannot escape the person he is, or give him the slip for long. With the shaving of the moustache goes the new identity, the mask. Guy is again open to the censure of his conscience; and the spiritual dryness that has accompanied him since his divorce again envelops him. The disguise had been a good one. It had made him feel that he belonged in the world, that he was not one singled out. The middle-aged man, humorous, whimsical, slightly ridiculous, reappears. Nevertheless, this individual carries within himself an assurance that will never desert him. The simple, unobtrusive man, looking for nothing in life save contentment, has temporarily found a useful

job to do. In his dedication to his country, a dedication that
corresponds to the romantic adventures of the nursery and
the school, he has captured some of the happiness he had
missed in his childhood. There is something more than
pathetic about Guy; he verges on the tragic. He excites the
humanity of the reader, who feels his innocence as a part of
the structure of society. And it is Waugh's comic sense that
keeps him humorous, likeable, human.

Guy, nevertheless, proceeds about his seduction. Virginia
is puzzled as to how he can allow himself the luxury of sin-
ning with her when he has told her that he is more religious
now than ever he was when she knew him. Twice, in Truslove fashion, Guy is near accomplishing his mission when he
is interrupted by the insistent ring of the telephone. It is
Apthorpe. Guy puts him off as curtly as he can. Finally
Virginia insists that Guy defend his position in wishing to
sin with her. He explains that according to Catholic theology
they are still married. Virginia had been impressed by the
man who had called her a tart; she is revolted by the man
who would sleep with her because he considers her still his
wife. To be made ridiculous by Guy's innocent and unknow-
ing cruelty is more than her nature will allow:

> "I thought you'd taken a fancy for me again and wanted
> a bit of fun for the sake of old times. I thought you'd
> chosen me specially, and by God you had. Because I was
> the only woman in the whole world your priests would
> let you go to bed with. You wet, smug, obscene, pom-
> pous, sexless lunatic pig." [*Men at Arms*, 164]

With this outburst comes Apthorpe's final call: "I say,
Crouchback, old man, I'm in something of a quandary. I've
just put a man under close arrest." [*Men at Arms*, 164] This
is what Virginia has done to Guy—she has put him under
arrest to his own conscience. This stain will remain, for Guy's
choice had been conscious. Theologically he is in the clear,

since in the eyes of the Church she is still his wife. But Virginia is not his wife in spirit. She has forfeited that right, and Guy has not thought of her as his wife for eight years. To demand the privileges of a husband would be to demand the right of property; it would be spiritually degrading. For though in his innocence Guy does realize this, he would be making a pander out of God. Virginia is quite correct when she says, "I was the only woman in the world your priests would let you go to bed with." However, Guy is saved from the action, for God cannot be served in dishonor.

God's providence makes itself apparent through Apthorpe, tenuously. One remembers how often in the course of the novel Waugh insists on the supernatural order in the phenomenal world. The opportune phone rings may imply the hand of God; at any rate they are brilliantly woven into the scene. Divine grace will not allow Guy to degrade himself and *not* sin, for he does not see, as Virginia does, the obscenity of the situation. He does not possess her acquaintance with evil. The fact that Virginia is a tart whom he is seducing, not the wife whom he honorably loves, makes all the difference.

The situation is not clearly defined theologically because the considerations seem primarily ethical. The issue is an uncomfortable one, saved only by the ridiculous remark of Apthorpe that he has put a civilian under military arrest. The scene seems to be Waugh's attempt to fuse the comic and the religious. He is, however, not completely successful. For the events assume the proportions of dilemma: Guy cannot sink to ethical degradation and remain theologically pure. His religion is shown to be the factor that sets him apart from the rest of the world. He feels no resentment for Apthorpe and Virginia; he feels only a deep sinking of the spirit, and he appreciates the ridiculous aspects of the situation: "Sir Roger, maybe, had felt thus when he drew his dedicated sword in a local brawl, not foreseeing that one day he would acquire that title of 'il Santo Inglese.'" [*Men at Arms*, 211] Waugh's attempt to explain the dilemma lies in the following quotation. Guy had said to his Halberdier Chaplain when slightly drunk:

> ". . . Do you agree . . . that the Supernatural Order is not something added to the Natural Order, like music or painting, to make everyday life more tolerable? It *is* everyday life. The Supernatural is real; what we call 'real' is mere shadow, a passing fancy." [*Men at Arms*, 89]

It is interesting to compare the two crucial situations in the novel: the one having to do with Guy's social life, the other with his spiritual welfare. When he finds himself reproved for having taken part in the African venture, for having taken the fatal bottle of whiskey to Apthorpe, Guy feels keenly a sense of disaster; but he knows that fundamentally he is not responsible for these calamities. He knows that they will leave no scar. When he thinks of the attempted seduction of his wife, he feels shame, the shame that he has always associated with sin. The sense of sin makes all the difference to him. And the shame that he feels reflects his moral integrity. He need not account for the actions of the world. The innocence which characterizes Guy is a potent one and his compassion ironic. The reader feels an essential kinship with the man.

Paul Pennyfeather and Adam Symes had been Waugh's link with the real world in the earlier works. But where they had been flat, though fascinating, characters, Guy is real. What rounds out his characterization is the religious element. Paul and Adam had wondered about the inconsistencies they had observed in the distorted world Waugh had put them into; but Guy need not wonder—he knows that all can be referred to God. Paradoxically, his religion is at once the source of his strength and that which sets him apart from his fellows. So much a Catholic is Crouchback that, when he dreams he is falling from a great height, he automatically makes an act of contrition.

In *Men at Arms* Waugh seems at ease with his religious theme, although he navigates some turbulent waters. He is able to use it to advantage to make satirical commentary on situations which are basically comic. He is able to strengthen the spirit of comedy and use it for moral emphasis. In the earlier novels the gusto and the enthusiasm of the comic spirit had pervaded to such an extent that they seemed to cut out the moral implications. The humor tended to exist by virtue of its spontaneity and inventiveness, and such a critic as Edmund Wilson put it down to snobbery, malicious wit and little else. In *Men at Arms,* as in *Brideshead Revisited* and *Helena,* Waugh is preoccupied with the religious considerations of his theme. Through his hero he traces the workings of divine grace on the individual soul; and by doing so in situations that are essentially comic, he succeeds in the comic situation. Wit and humor become allies of morality.

Men at Arm was originally intended to be the first part of a trilogy dealing with the years of war. *Officers and Gentlemen*[23] (1955) is the second volume to deal with the events of the war up to the time of Russia's participation. Waugh had originally thought that it would take him three volumes to develop his themes, but he discovered, as a note appended to *Officers and Gentlemen* indicates, that two would do the trick. (Waugh goes on to state that he has not abandoned the characters introduced in *Men at Arms* and developed farther in the sequel, that in later novels he intends to follow their fortunes in later episodes of the war.)

Officers and Gentlemen continues to trace the disillusionment of Guy Crouchback in his return to England after the African escapade with Ben Ritchie-Hook and the death of Apthorpe, on a search of Apthorpe's heir, Chatty Corner, then on a mission to Alexandria and finally on a retreat from the island of Crete. But the sequel to *Men at Arms* is not a success. It lacks the warm intimacy of its predecessor, and it fails to maintain an interest in the characters that had earlier appeared so brilliant in conception. Furthermore, Waugh's desire to fuse the religious theme and the comic method seems to have deserted him; for Crouchback, the hero who had gone out to fight the war for England and Saint George, is now described as a man "who without deliberation had begun to dissociate himself from the army in matters of real concern."[23] The "glory and dedication" that Guy identifies with the cause of England at war have dimmed and soured; and the brotherhood that had so characterized the men at arms of the earlier volume has proved illusory. Nor does Waugh find it profitable to develop further the theme that "the Supernatural Order is not something added to the Natural Order, like music or painting, to make everyday life more tolerable[?] It *is* everyday life" [*Men at Arms*, 89].

Periodically, Waugh makes mention of the religious seasons: Pentecost, All Souls Day, Lent; but the notes struck do not form a convincing background for the monotonous and unconvincing movements of the action. Guy Crouchback's dedication to God and country seems to him a mockery, and he moves from one disillusionment to another still more keen.

The satire is aimed at the army; it is not the gentle remonstrance that characterized the earlier book. Rather it is a contemptuous and biting appraisal of incompetence and bad management. Waugh delights in describing the confusion engendered by a power force moving without clear objective or design; he delights in the irony of Trimmer—one-time hairdresser—ascending to the hallowed precincts of heroism, and the prostitution of Guy's wife, Virginia, to the ideal "new Englishman" as portrayed by Trimmer. A plangent note is struck as Waugh describes the defection of

Crouchback's idol Ivor Claire who, rather than remain on Crete as orders indicate, escapes to Alexandria. Having the incriminating documents in his possession, Guy, after a siege of extreme melancholy, decides to burn them, thus dissociating himself further from that army in which he had thought to find purpose and meaning in his unhappy life. Crouchback understands the atrocity of war as he stands over the body of the young soldier, and he humanely takes the dog tags from the boy's neck so that his parents, and the army, may be notified of the death. But the dog tags, entrusted to Julia Stitch, find their way into a wastebasket.

There is an attempt made in the novel to show the simultaneity of events. While Guy is busy on Crete and in Alexandria, the reader is given glimpses of Trimmer having greatness thrust upon him; the elder Crouchback teaching his form, playing games; Virginia, perhaps the last of the Bright Young People, moving aimlessly from lover to lover, vainly trying to disembarrass herself of Trimmer.

In the journal of Corporal-Major Lodovic, Waugh occasionally introduces a serious note: an observer of some discrimination, Lodovic aptly describes Guy as a romantic who would like to believe that the war is being fought by gentlemen. True as this may be, it is not enough to raise the novel to the same level of excellence as its predecessor. Like most sequels, *Officers and Gentlemen* suffers by comparison. It neither pleases nor satisfies. Yet it will be interesting to watch for Crouchback in subsequent novels and to see what use, if any, Waugh makes of his theme of the supernatural order in the natural order.

Chapter 7

Conclusions

In *Brideshead Revisited* Waugh succeeded in detaching himself from the comic convention that distinguished his earlier work and moved into the dimensions of the traditional novel. Here he scored brilliantly. From the stuff of his own religious convictions he erected an apologia for the Roman Catholic faith in England. The apologetic note which some have labelled a weakness is really one of the novel's strengths; for completely integrated with the apology is the theme: divine grace manifesting itself in the real world, pulling back into the faith God's own by a twitch upon the thread. In *Brideshead Revisited* Waugh demonstrated the supernatural order in the world. Sebastian Flyte's entire revolt is to be put down to his refusal to accept the promptings of grace. His sister, Cordelia, makes the point clearly when she tells Charles Ryder that Sebastian had always had a vocation and hated it. But grace brings him back into the Church. Sebastian's innocence, indeed, protects his essential goodness.

In *Men at Arms* Waugh implies again the supernatural in the phenomenal world. Divine grace again exerts its pressures to keep Crouchback theologically pure. In *Brideshead Revisited,* however, the sermonizing and the insistence on the religious theme tend to make the novel an intellectual masterpiece first, an experience of life second. *Brideshead Revisited* is a magnificent *tour de force,* extremely sensitive in its evaluation of human motives. If it has a fault it is that Waugh over-insists on its emotional validity. In *Helena*, it is Waugh's insistence on religious history and Church matters that removes it from his usual range of excellence. He fails time and again to appeal to the emotions of his reader. *Helena* is not a convincing portrait of an inquisitive young girl who eventually becomes a saint, although it is supposed to be just this. It is, instead, the portrayal of an era of Christian history, one that primarily interests an apologist for Church actions. Waugh attempts to imply a parallel situation with modern times, and certainly Constantius Chlorus and Constantine the Great bear resemblances to the power addict of today. But *Helena* fails as a novel because it displays neither the intellectual strength of *Brideshead Revisited* nor the comic brilliance of *Men at Arms*.

All of this leads to the conclusion that Waugh is not completely at home in the confines of the traditionally serious novel. It is in the comic novel that he triumphs. And in *Men at Arms* his comic brilliance is seen to advantage. The reader knows that Crouchback is a Catholic; but his Catholicism is just one facet of his character, albeit the important one. One feels that it is an adjunct to a basic innocence that forever manifests itself. Crouchback's religion is the standard of measurement from which one judges his actions. *Men at Arms* is a fine story—the theological implications are completely integrated into the plot. The comic invention is as brilliant and funny as ever, although it seems touched by a melancholy that accompanies Guy wherever he goes. The novel succeeds in creating a picture of the complete and utter illogicality a soldier comes to identify with war. The plot moves rapidly and halts dismally as Waugh describes the tempo of army life in garrison, on board ship and in maneuvers. In his description of his men at arms, Waugh has succeeded in defining the essential nature of the British soldier. There is Major Tickeridge, solid and dependable, somewhat wistful, somewhat sad; Leonard, the wife-ridden young man who is killed by a bomb in London after refusing to sail with the regiment; Sarum-Smith who takes infinite delight in executing meaningless details; and Trimmer, the incompetent. There is Ben Ritchie-Hook, the Brigadier. A modification of Captain Hook in *Peter Pan,* he is the *enfant terrible* of the First World War, the roué of the twenties, and the infantile general of the forties. It is, however, the fusion of the comic and the religious that makes *Men at Arms* the best of Waugh's novels. It is a comic, somewhat melancholy, account of innocence abroad in an evil world of blundering men.

What the religious theme amounts to, finally, in Waugh's work is this: it is his answer to the ills of the waste land which he had so admirably defined in his early novels. In his own Roman Catholicism he found a measure of hope. In his novels he has sought to define this hope. For Waugh and for his heroes it is a light constantly burning before a tabernacle. It is the permanence that all his Bright Young People sought for.

Bibliography

Maritain, Jacques and Jean Cocteau, *Art and Faith*. New York: Philosophical Library, 1948.

——, *Art and Scholasticism*. New York: Scribners, 1949.

——, *Man and the State*. Chicago: University of Chicago Press, 1951.

McSorley, Joseph, Review of *Brideshead Revisited, Catholic World, CLXII* (February, 1946), 469–470.

Newby, P. H., *The Novel: 1945–1950*. London: Longmans, Green, 1951.

O'Donnell, Donat, *Maria Cross: Imaginative Patterns in a Group of Catholic Writers*. New York: Oxford, 1952.

Rajan, B., ed., *Focus One*. London: Dennis Dobson, 1945.

Savage, D. S., "The Innocence of Evelyn Waugh," *Focus Four,* ed. B. Rajan. London: Dennis Dobson, 1947, 34–45.

Schwartz, Delmore, "Long After Eden," *The Partisan Review,* XIX (November, December, 1952), 703–704.

Temple, P., "Some Sidelights on Evelyn Waugh," *America,* LXXV (April 27, 1946), 75–76.

Tindall, William York, *Forces in Modern British Literature: 1885–1946*. New York: Knopf, 1947.

Voorhees, R. J., "Evelyn Waugh Revisited," *South Atlantic Quarterly,* L (July, 1951), 389–398.

Waugh, Evelyn, "American Epoch in the Catholic Church, *Life,* XXVII (September 19, 1949), 134–137.

——, *Bachelor Abroad: A Mediterranean Journey*. New York: Farrar, Straus, 1930.

——, *Black Mischief* (Uniform Edition). London: Chapman and Hall, 1948.

——, *Brideshead Revisited* (Uniform Edition). London: Chapman and Hall, 1949.

——, "Come Inside," *The Road to Damascus*, ed. John A. O'Brien. Garden City: Doubleday, 1949, 15–20.

——, "Death in Hollywood," *Life*, XXXIII (September 29, 1947), 73–74.

——, *Decline and Fall* (Uniform Edition). London: Chapman and Hall, 1949.

——, *Edmund Campion*. London: Longmans, Green, 1935.

——, "Felix Culpa?" *Commonweal*, LIV (August 17, 1951), 454.

——, *Helena*. London: Chapman and Hall, 1950.

——, "Love Among the Ruins," *Commonweal*, LVIII (July 31, 1953), 410–422.

——, *The Loved One*. New York: Grosset and Dunlap, 1948.

——, *Men at Arms*. London: Chapman and Hall, 1951.

——, *Mexican Object Lesson*. London: Chapman and Hall, 1940.

——, *Ninety-two Days: The Account of a Tropical Journey through British Guiana and Brazil*. New York: Farrar, Straus, 1934.

——, *Officers and Gentlemen*. London: Chapman and Hall, 1955.

——, *Put Out More Flags* (Uniform Edition). London: Chapman and Hall, 1951.

——, *Remote People*. London: Duckworth, 1931.

——, *Scoop* (Uniform Edition). London: Chapman and Hall, 1951.

——, *Scott-King's Modern Europe*. Boston: Little, Brown, 1949.

——, *Vile Bodies* (Uniform Edition). London: Chapman and Hall, 1949.

——, *Waugh in Abyssinia*. Toronto: Longmans, Green, 1936.

——, *When the Going Was Good*. Boston: Little, Brown, 1947.

——, *Work Suspended and Other Stories* (Uniform Edition). London: Chapman and Hall, 1950.

Wilson, Edmund, *Classics and Commercials: A Literary Chronicle of the Forties*. New York: Farrar and Straus, 1950.

Footnotes

1. Evelyn Waugh, *Brideshead Revisited* (London, 1949), 76–77. Hereafter known as *Brideshead Revisited*.
2. Graham Greene, "Francois Mauriac," *The Lost Childhood* (London, 1951), 69.
3. T. S. Eliot, *After Strange Gods* (London, 1934), 54. Hereafter known as *After Strange Gods*.
4. William York Tindall, *Forces in Modern British Literature: 1885–1946* (New York, 1947), 122. Hereafter known as Tindall.
5. Andre Gide, *Journals*, Vol. III: *1928–1939* (New York, 1949), 259. Hereafter known as *Journals*.
6. Jacques Maritain, *Art and Scholasticism* (New York, 1949), 171. Hereafter known as Maritain.
7. Evelyn Waugh, "Come Inside," *The Road to Damascus: The Spiritual Pilgrimage of Fifteen Converts to Catholicism*, ed. John A. O'Brien (Garden City, 1949), 20.
8. These beliefs of Waugh are found in more explicit statement in his life of Edmund Campion which was first published in September, 1935.
9. Evelyn Waugh, *Decline and Fall* (London, 1949), 232–233. Hereafter known as *Decline and Fall*.
10. D. S. Savage, "The Innocence of Evelyn Waugh," *Focus Four: The Novelist as Thinker*, ed. B. Rajan (London, 1947), 34–35. Hereafter known as Savage.
11. Edmund Wilson, *Classics and Commercials: A Literary Chronicle of the Forties* (New York, 1950), 146. Hereafter known as Wilson. *Classics and Commercials* is a collection of essays originally published in *The New Yorker* and other magazines.
12. Evelyn Waugh, *Vile Bodies* (London, 1949), 126–127. Hereafter known as *Vile Bodies*.
13. Evelyn Waugh, *Black Mischief* (London, 1948), 142. Hereafter known as *Black Mischief*.
14. Evelyn Waugh, *A Handful of Dust* (London, 1949), 123. Hereafter known as *A Handful of Dust*.
15. Evelyn Waugh, *Scoop* (London, 1951), 43–44. Hereafter known as *Scoop*.
16. Evelyn Waugh, *Put Out More Flags* (London, 1951), 11. Hereafter known as *Put Out More Flags*.

17. Joseph McSorley, Review of *Brideshead Revisited, The Catholic World,* CLXII (Feb. 1946), 469–470.

18. Evelyn Waugh, "Death in Hollywood," *Life* XXIII (Sept. 29, 1947), 73. Hereafter known as *Life.*

19. Evelyn Waugh, *The Loved One* (New York, 1948), 163. Hereafter known as *The Loved One.*

20. Evelyn Waugh, *Scott-King's Modern Europe* (Boston, 1949), 89.

21. Evelyn Waugh, *Helena* (London, 1950), ix. Hereafter known as *Helena.*

22. Evelyn Waugh, *Men at Arms* (London, 1952), 13. Hereafter known as *Men at Arms.*

23. Evelyn Waugh, *Officers and Gentlemen* (London, 1955), p. 161.